Books to change your life and work.
Accessible, easy to read and easy to act on –
other titles in the **How To** series include:

Writing an Essay
How to improve your performance in coursework and examinations

Critical Thinking for Students
How to assess arguments and effectively present your own

Writing Your Dissertation
How to plan, prepare and present successful work

Writing an Assignment
How to improve your research and presentation skills

Polish Up Your Punctuation and Grammar
Master the basics of the English language and write with greater confidence

The *How To series* now contains
around 200 titles in the following categories:

Business & Management
Career Choices
Career Development
Computers & the Net
Creative Writing
Home & Family
Living & Working Abroad
Personal Development
Personal Finance
Self-Employment & Small Business
Study Skills & Student Guides

For full details, please send to our distributors for a free copy of the latest catalogue:

How To Books
Customer Services Dept.
Plymbridge Distributors Ltd, Estover Road
Plymouth PL6 7PZ, United Kingdom
Tel: 01752 202301   Fax: 01752 202331
http://www.howtobooks.co.uk

Passing Exams Without Anxiety

*How to get organised, prepare yourself
and feel confident of success*

DAVID ACRES
5th edition

How To Books

Published by How To Books Ltd,
3 Newtec Place, Magdalen Road,
Oxford OX4 1RE. United Kingdom.
Tel: (01865) 793806. Fax: (01865) 248780.
email: info@howtobooks.co.uk
www.howtobooks.co.uk

Fifth edition 1998
Reprinted 2000

British Library Cataloguing in Publication Data
A catalogue record for this book is available from
the British Library

Consultant Editor – Roland Seymour

Cartoons by Mike Flanagan
Cover design by Shireen Nathoo Design
Cover image PhotoDisc
Cover copy by Sallyann Sheridan

Produced for How To Books by Deer Park Productions
Typeset by PDQ Typesetting, Stoke-on-Trent, Staffs.
Printed and bound by The Cromwell Press, Trowbridge,
Wiltshire

NOTE: The material contained in this book is set out in good
faith for general guidance and no liability can be accepted
for loss or expense incurred as a result of relying in particular
circumstances on statements made in the book. Laws and
regulations are complex and liable to change, and readers should
check the current position with the relevant authorities before
making personal arrangements.

Contents

List of Illustrations   7

Preface to the fifth edition   8

1 Using this book   11

Creating the time to use this book   11
Asking questions: the most important skill   12
Making the most of yourself   16
Achieving success: five factors   17
Using the ideas in this book   18

2 Tackling the coursework deadlines   20

Overcoming the problem of deadlines   20
Tackling the problems of coursework   20
Checklist: your coursework problems   21
Choosing where to study   27
Organising storage space   29
Keeping your motivation alive   32
Keeping track of time   36
Using computers to help with your studies   41
Getting help in using computers   43

3 Organising your revision   44

Reviewing and revising   44
Checklist: your revision problems   45
Planning your revision   47
Organising your revision time   58
How to revise   61

4 Improving your memory   71

Learning more about memory   71
Checklist: your memory problems   72

Choosing ways of remembering 73
Creating a better memory 75
Using your brain: right and left halves 78
Using all your senses 79
Matching techniques to your senses 81
Making word and letter associations 88
Revising and remembering for problem-solving science and technology subjects 91
Understanding and remembering Maths 92
Wanting to know more? 94

5   Taking exams   95

Minimising exam difficulties 95
Knowing your examinations 96
Making contingency plans 96
Checklist: your exam problems 98
Getting used to exams 101
Dispelling irrational beliefs about exams 105
Using the last few hours 108
Starting your exam 110
Understanding the types of question 114
Overcoming common exam problems 121
Coping with the aftermath 122

6   Coping with anxiety   124

Understanding worry, anxiety and stress 124
Checklist: your anxiety problems 125
Reducing stressful thinking 130
Coping with stressful situations 136
Coping with key times 140
Getting to sleep at night 142
Breathing effectively 149
Relaxing your muscles 152
Visualising 160
Finding other approaches 164

7   Using others as helpers   167

Negotiating help 167
Talking about your problem 170
Using more than one helper for revision 172

Glossary 174
Further reading 176
Useful addresses 179
Index 180

List of Illustrations

1	The underlining technique	15
2	A time chart	38
3	A simple symbol system	48
4	Spider diagrams	54
5	A sample mind map	57
6	A weekly time chart	62
7	An outline revision card	65
8	Aids to visual technique	82
9	Using eyes for recall	86, 87
10	Recording exam information	97
11	What examiners want	106
12	Techniques in the exam room	112
13	Stress reduction checklist	131
14	Sleeping and relaxation positions	147
15	Breathing exercises	149
16	A guide to muscular relaxation	154
17	Your relaxation programme	155

Preface
to the 5th edition

'Passing exams *without* anxiety?' is the first sceptical question that is asked about this book. The answer to the question is 'Yes' and the success of this book is due, in large part, to the fact that it contains the solutions to problems offered by hundreds of students tackling every form of examination. These range from school-based tests, GCSEs and A levels to vocational and professional qualifications, degrees and postgraduate qualifications.

Here you will find ways to tackle coursework and revision by using the ideas of students who have converted panic and anxiety into focused energy and used this energy to be successful in exams. You will find hundreds of ideas to help you transform nervous anxiety into a balanced, positive approach to coursework, revision and exams.

The fifth edition has been completely revised and made even easier to read and use. The new ideas added to the last edition include extra guidelines on the use of computers and portfolios; more tips for GCSE students and ideas for part-time students or those returning to study. Parents of students and teachers will find tips on how they can be helpful throughout the book and especially in Chapter 7.

I would like to thank all those who have so generously offered their time and ideas over the years. For this fifth edition, I would particularly like to thank Sandra Graham and Sylvia Thomas for their detailed comments and suggested amendments to the text. In addition, they have contributed examples of their experiences as students who successfully returned to study. It is difficult to acknowledge everybody by name but I would like to mention those who have contributed specific examples and who have made helpful contributions to the text: John Acres, Kate Acres, Gail Cann, Roger Catchpole, Anna Fahdi, John Jenkinson (for his figure drawings), Jo McCaren, Guy Nelson and the sixth-formers of Sackville School (East Grinstead), Margaret Oliver, Roma Thomas, Colin Richman, Wendy Trott, Carol Turley, Katherine Turner, Cathy Warburton and Kevin

Westmancott. Finally I would like to acknowledge the contribution of Roland Seymour who first saw the potential for this book and has supported its development through to this fifth edition.

David Acres

IS THIS YOU?

Returner to study

GCSE candidate   A level candidate

College student

Part-time student   GNVQ student

Postgraduate

Crafts student   Undergraduate

Doing an access course

Distance learner   Mature student

Sitting an oral exam or viva

Studying for Highers   Professional student

Taking an S/NVQ

Studying humanities   Studying science/technology

Reviser

Essay writer   Doing a project

Preparing a dissertation

Overseas student   Exam re-taker

Diploma student

Applying for a place   Applying for a scholarship

Civil service candidate

Teacher   Lecturer

Student counsellor

Tutor   Librarian

Taking a test

1
Using this Book

CREATING THE TIME TO USE THIS BOOK

You can use this book any time you have five minutes or more to spare. If you feel that you cannot spare five minutes, then pick another time when you feel less pressured. Although in reality you could probably create the time, it is probably anxiety which contributes towards your feeling that you do not have enough time.

In five minutes or so, you can:

- read the back cover, the Preface to the fifth edition and the list of contents

- use the time to spot whether the book appears to have some content relevant to you and to note chapters of interest to you

- jot down a question or two that you would hope the book could help you answer.

In another fifteen minutes or so, you can:

- read the section on **Asking questions** (page 12), which is in many ways the most important section to understand if you want to make the best use of this – or any books and notes you read

- write down any question you have as you read through the **Checklists** (pages 21, 45, 72, 96, 125) or the chapters that seem most relevant

- note down useful tips as you find them in the checklists as well as the relevant page numbers. Then look up the relevant pages in the chapter.

1. If you can't find what you are looking for in the index, flip through the pages of the chapter(s) you feel are likely to be most relevant.

2. Keep your questions next to you and look for pages that may be relevant to them.

3. Be methodical in writing down the pages you note that look useful.

You can use short bursts like this any time you visit the book with a particular question in mind.

Picking relevant parts of this book

This book is not written to be read from cover to cover. You don't have enough time to spend hours reading books about how to study and pass exams in addition to your subject studies. So pick and choose the parts of this book which appear to be most relevant to you.

This chapter explains how to find the ideas which are most relevant and useful to you; how to find them quickly and the key ideas to notice as you use the other chapters.

ASKING QUESTIONS: THE MOST IMPORTANT SKILL

I strongly recommend that you read through this book in exactly the same way as you should revise and take examinations – *with questions constantly in your mind*. Use these guidelines to develop your questioning techniques and then use them to *pick and choose the ideas which best seem to answer your questions*.

● Don't pick up this book after this moment without having a question in mind.

There are *two types of question* you should ask yourself continuously. The first type is about *the topic you are studying*, e.g. The First World War if you are studying History as a subject. The second type of question is about *you*: what you are doing and how you are proceeding when you are studying. *Both types of questions are of equal importance.*

Questioning the topic

You can find questions about a topic you are studying from:

● Old examination questions. These are usually obtainable from an examining board or through teachers, lecturers or libraries.
● Questions you have tried to answer during the course, e.g. essay questions.
● Any suggestions or guidelines given to you by teachers, lecturers or tutors.
● Talking to friends and sharing ideas.
● Your own interests, the things you want to know.

- The work you have studied during the year, indicated by headings in your notes. You can convert these topic headings into questions by using questions beginning with the six key words in the Kipling poem, i.e. What? When? Why? How? Where? Who? You would need to choose a topic and then see if you can think of a question beginning with any of those six words.

Example
Using the History topic, The First World War, I constructed six questions:

What..were the main causes?
When .... was the turning point of the war?
Why .... were the casualties so enormous?
How .... was Germany made to pay at the end of the war?
Where .... were the principal battlefields?
Who ...... were the politicians principally responsible for the war?

You will need to construct the same sort of topic questions in order to use this book. Some useful questions about this book and the topics within it would include:

- What problems have I got with studying for exams?
- Why do I get so nervous and what can I do about it?
- How can reading this book solve my revision problems?
- Where should I revise?
- Who should I use to help me – and how?
- To what subjects do these ideas apply?
- How difficult would it be to try this idea?
- When should I start my revision?

Questioning yourself
These are questions you ask yourself in order to keep a watchful eye on how you are spending your time; whether you know what you are doing and why you are doing it. Some useful questions to ask yourself when using this book would include:

- What am I reading this page for?
- Why am I looking at this book?
- What do I want to find out?
- Where shall I look next?
- Have I understood what I have just read?
- When will I be justified in taking a break?
- Am I concentrating?

- What will I do immediately after I have finished this?
- What is the time?

Example

I looked in the kitchen cupboard for the soluble aspirin, without success. They had all gone. Two minutes later I searched unsuccessfully for some sugar in another cupboard. I returned to the first cupboard to continue the search and found it immediately on the same shelf on which I'd searched for the aspirin. I had not 'seen' it before, even though I probably touched it, even moved it, in my search for the soluble aspirin. It was another reminder to me that if I know what I'm looking for I'm likely to find it.

I'd guess that you are likely to recall similar incidents. The relevance to study is that your questions (what you are looking for) are much more likely to produce answers (the discovery of the sugar).

You will notice that not all the questions (see above) have to begin with the six key words. It is the principle of questioning that is, and has been, so fundamental in learning for hundreds and, indeed, thousands of years – Socrates was promoting the value of question and answer in ancient Greece (Socratic dialogue). The particular value of it has been expressed well by Rudyard Kipling in 'The Elephant's Child':

I keep six honest serving-men
They taught me all I knew
Their names are What and Why and When
And How and Where and Who.

Making up questions

You can try this by opening any book or set of notes and finding a *heading or sub-heading* on a page. I opened up this book and found the heading **Revising effectively** (page 46) and tried peppering the heading using the guidelines from **Asking questions**.

What makes for efficient revision?
How many features are there of efficient revision?
What's my most efficient time for revision?
When do I feel most efficient revising?
What is different from what I would do already?
Why change what I am doing already?

You can also use the *first or last sentence of paragraphs* to generate these types of question even when there is no sub-heading like 'Revising effectively'.

If you practise both of these techniques you will become a more active learner. Then you can use the technique as part of your regular study habits whether during your coursework, assignments or preparing for exams.

Using this approach for assignment questions

The key to answering any question (even one you have set yourself) is to clearly understand precisely what it is asking you to do.

This usually means that you have to spend time, even slowly – analysing it *actively* by yourself, with a friend or both.

You can do this by the underlining technique shown in Figure 1 and you can couple this with a technique which I call 'peppering' or 'bombarding' the question with little questions. Some of these useful little questions are:

What does this mean?
How is this defined?
What is this?
Do I understand this?

Rudyard Kipling's 'honest serving-men' also help (see above).

Example

To demonstrate this technique, I have both underlined and 'peppered' the question on Figure 1. As I did so, I spoke aloud talking to myself

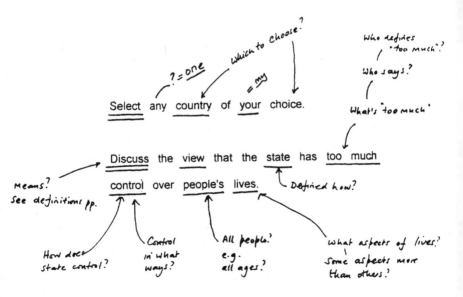

Fig. 1. The underlining technique.

about each aspect of the question so that it was clear to me.

Having done this, I can use these 'little' questions to help me to set off with my reading. Later they will be helpful to enable me to structure the answer to the assignment. Initially, though, I can attempt to answer each question by jotting down my own first ideas, in a list, a spider-diagram or pattern. I can then go off and ask questions about other aspects of the assignment with some knowledge or understanding of my own with which to build a link – I can see an *association* between what I know and what I want to know.

• As an extra tip, carry cards, bookmarks or Post-its (page 34) with these questions on, to keep you focused on the relevant issues when you are reading, thinking and note taking.

MAKING THE MOST OF YOURSELF

Choosing the ideas that suit you

There is no one perfect or correct way of revising or taking examinations. There are numerous ideas that work. Select those ideas you feel would suit you and your needs. Add them to any ways you have for studying already that you want to retain.

It is worth noting that it is often difficult to change your old habits, your old ways of doing things. Even if they don't seem to work very well, at least they are known to you, familiar, i.e. 'The devil you know rather than the devil you don't know'. My experience is that it is worth changing at least some of your old ways. It is likely you are already using some of the ideas in this book if you are studying effectively. If you are not using any of the ideas in this book, I'd be very surprised if you are studying effectively.

Bear in mind that new ideas often need a little practice. Sometimes, like any new skills, your performance may be less effective for a very short time, before you see the real benefits. Having said that this may occur, the opposite is true of many of these ideas: you will see immediate improvement in performance.

Making the most of your ability

Ability, hard work and determination have seen thousands of students successfully through the exam system – but not necessarily. Anxiety affects people of all abilities. Among the people I have met who are most anxious about their examinations are large numbers who have gained Upper Second Class and First Class Honours degrees.

There is a belief that those who do well in examinations are those who have ability, work hard and are determined characters. Expressed as a sum, it would be

ABILITY + DETERMINATION + HARD WORK = ACHIEVEMENT

I would have difficulty in marking this sum, as I believe it is incomplete. Correct as it may be for many candidates, it is certainly inadequate as an explanation of the achievements of many others.

Two examples of this are:

- Those whose ability appears to produce achievement without hard work or determination. This is a category of candidate who is often referred to, but is, I suspect, less common than supposed. This candidate makes others feel sick!

- Those whose determination and hard work overcome their apparent lack of ability. In my first year of teaching I met Charlie, a year 10 student who had a measured IQ of 71. He later successfully took Science O levels, A level Chemistry and went on to higher education. As at the time it was supposedly a borderline decision as to whether he then went to a special school or not, this *both* demonstrated to me the value of an absorbing interest, hard work and determination *and* commented upon the value of categorising by a single number a human being's ability to learn.

ACHIEVING SUCCESS: FIVE FACTORS

Achievement is the sum not of three but of five factors. They are:

1. *Ability*
Whilst there are obvious limits to an individual's ability to achieve in particular areas of activity, I believe that much ability of the most able to the least able remains untapped and under-developed. Further, I believe most candidates can considerably improve their performance in examinations and that the vast majority who are entered for a particular exam have, at the very least, the ability to *pass* it. With better *technique*, most candidates would be gaining more marks.

2. *Determination and motivation*
Determination is a very useful trait, if it is channelled and focused in the appropriate direction. I have met very determined people who have studied in entirely inappropriate ways and as a result exhausted themselves and marred their exam performance. However, assuming that you choose the techniques which bring out the best in you, your own motivation to succeed is an extremely important element in meeting your goals.

3. Work rate
I've met large number of candidates who have worked very hard but inefficiently and whose performance in examinations has been a surprise and disappointment both to themselves and their teachers, families and friends. Hard work should bring achievement when coupled with efficient and appropriate revision and exam techniques. Indeed most students should be able to achieve satisfactory standards without hard work, if their techniques are good.

4. Technique
You will achieve success if you choose the techniques and approaches which most suit you as a person: this book is packed with these tips and ideas.

5. Coping with yourself as a person
Success in examinations is not just a matter of using your thinking or intellectual ability. It is also dependent upon your feelings and behaviour. In particular how you cope with the potentially bewildering tasks you aim to complete; how you cope with any past experiences of learning and taking exams (frequently negative); how you cope with your own or other people's expectations and how you cope with any anxiety you experience, are often just as important as ability. This is the reason for a **coping with anxiety** section being incorporated with **organising your revision** and **taking exams** in this book.
My revised sum would be:

ABILITY + DETERMINATION + WORK RATE + TECHNIQUE + COPING WITH YOURSELF = ACHIEVEMENT

USING THE IDEAS IN THIS BOOK
You need to choose the ideas which you feel you can use at this particular time and place, as well as the methods that suit you.

Example: writing this book
I have used a great many ideas which you'll find in this book in order to write it. These include:

- Short periods of time to nibble away at the task.

- Post-it notes to record quick thoughts or mark useful material.

- Walked and drank fresh water to revive me when I flagged.

- Plastic envelopes to keep all linked material together.

- A new study area where I felt comfortable to write: I cleared my desk of clutter.

- Used two critical 'friends' to check and criticise previous editions of the book.

- Asked other people to contribute their ideas.

- Looked for new ideas in TV programmes and magazines.

- Listened to music that relaxed me.

- In writing the fifth edition, I changed a number of ways that I worked, e.g. I did not work in a library. These methods suited me in a way that they did not previously.

You can pick and choose the ideas in this book, adopting the techniques which suit you. You can also amend them, after trying them out, to ensure you feel confident you are using the technique in the way that fits your natural ways of approaching tasks.

2
Tackling Coursework Deadlines

OVERCOMING THE PROBLEM OF DEADLINES

It is not just exams which can generate anxiety when you are studying. Many students find that coursework and coursework deadlines can be just as difficult to manage. There can be problems in tackling several assignments for different subjects at the same time. Projects can prove difficult to start and/or to complete. In further and higher education you can meet up with tests at the end of short courses or modules, which count towards your overall diploma or degree performance.

From GCSE onwards, more courses in sixth forms, further and higher education have coursework as an important component in the overall assessment. The percentage of coursework marks that count in the final assessment can vary from 100 per cent to 0 per cent. Forty per cent is a common average, although in subjects like English and Mathematics at GCSE level that percentage is likely to be no more than 30 per cent or 20 per cent.

There can be many problems to overcome when tackling coursework and the Checklist on page 21 can help you identify the parts of this chapter and other chapters which can help you solve them.

But do not despair – problems are there to be overcome and here you will find dozens of ideas that other students have used to successfully meet coursework deadlines. The key solutions are often to do with how you organise both your time (when) and your place (where) of study, and here you will find ideas about both.

TACKLING THE PROBLEMS OF COURSEWORK

Have you left it too late?
Even if you feel you have left the coursework until too late, you probably have not as there are normally still some marks to be acquired. Providing you have not missed firm deadlines beyond which no marks can be obtained, you can rescue something from the mess you may feel you are in by a basic approach which means you can choose to:

CHECKLIST: YOUR COURSEWORK PROBLEMS

I have/may have problems with	Tick if it applies to you	Brief tips	Where to find out more (pages)
Leaving coursework until the last minute		Avoid running scared. Spend a few minutes – 5 or 10 – doing some small task connected with different coursework for a few days, it soon mounts up.	20–21 22—23
Getting started		Start at a time you're most alert and most relaxed picking something you find interesting, easy or understandable.	23–24
Organising myself		Find some permanent shelves or storage space for your paper; colour code what you want to find.	40–41 34
Motivating myself		Give yourself specific rewards for completing a short, easy or interesting task; work with a friend; change time and place to study.	23–24 168–169 38–39
Falling behind with a project		Talk over with someone what the problem is – identify it and start to nibble away at the separate tasks that make up a project or dissertation.	32–33
Organising my room		Do not work in a tip as you will probably feel messy; look at it afresh, move things around so it feels as right as it can.	29–30
Friends interrupting me		Opt for friends who cheer you up when they phone or call; negotiate some nights or time for study/some for social life – and remind them you both agreed.	168–169
Meeting deadlines		Keep dates pinned up on a board.	40–41
Falling behind with coursework		Divide time up between subjects, ticking off your time progress. Identify problems or blocks and seek help by changing your approach.	58–59 49–50
Balancing the amount of work I do for each subject		Tick off your progress in each subject, matching up the number of ticks.	49–50 51
Panic		Do a little often, talk to someone whom you find helpful about your worries; learn some techniques to stop panic. Learn the Emergency Panic technique.	149 164 168–169
Forgetting deadlines until the last moment		Try a wallchart with dates clearly indicated.	24
Deciding which coursework to tackle first		Use a simple prioritising system such as that used for revision; do not use urgency as the only deciding factor.	26–27 47–51
Finding the best time of day to study		Check the exercise provided and try to spot both your first and second best times of day (so you have a choice).	37–38
Finding enough time to study		There are 168 hours in a week, plenty of time for you to find around 20 hours spread over 7 days.	36–39 59
Finding the best place to study		Use the environment checklist to spot your best learning environment.	27–29

- *Do something*. The time for worrying is past; here is an opportunity to get on with it so take simple practical action such as find some facts; speak to someone; collect a book; talk to a tutor; photocopy some useful pages from a book and so on.

- Cut out the frills or anything but the essentials in what you write ('Cut the crap').

- Determine a clear line of approach – and stick to it.

- Use the **Deciding priority** list (page 49) to decide a starting point. Start with areas of highest appeal and that are most useful.

- Break the whole assignment down into 'bite size' bits or 'nibbles': tackle these one at a time.

- Pursue the answers to one or two vital questions, putting the other questions to one side initially.

- Write in short simple sentences, wasting the minimum time in forming words.

Feeling ready to study?

You can waste a lot of time at a desk trying to study unless you approach it in the right frame of mind. The following eight-point plan will help you check whether you are properly prepared to start out on an effective study session. (You can find a patterned note version of the points on page 57.)

1. Are you relaxed and composed?
Avoid starting the task in a state of anxiety. There are a number of suggestions for preparing yourself in the **Coping with Anxiety** chapter but a positive frame of mind, some physically relaxing movement before you start and some background music may all help.

2. Are you wanting to do it?
Check your motivation out by using the guidelines in **Motivating yourself** (page 23). *Wanting* to be studying that particular topic is a key to starting doing so.

3. Are you clear about what you are going to do?
You are ready when you have a specific one, two or three tasks in mind and some sense of the timescale attached to them, i.e. 'I will X by Y time'. Do not set artificially strict deadlines on yourself, for that way you may end up with a sense of failure, rather than success.

4. Have you got your questions ready?
This is to emphasise the point that we learn best those things that are answers to questions and that having a question or two in mind provides a valuable starting point. See **Asking questions** (page 12).

5. A 'feel good' place to study?
Feeling right about the study environment will enable you to settle to the task quickly, particularly if you have cleared the space of clutter. You can check out your best learning environment on pages 27–29.

6. Gather the material you need
Having the books, newspaper articles, handouts, notes, drawings, calculator or tape recorder by your study space will enable you to make a start, confident that you have sufficient reference material close at hand. This also assumes that you have familiarised yourself with how to use a library and other electronic equipment that can help you find or use material. If you have not, then identify what you need to know and ask someone with the know-how to show you the practical steps you can take. If you build up your confidence in information gathering, it will spread to other study tasks.

7. Pick the right time of day
Some routine tasks that require little concentration or energy fit into your low-energy times of day once you have identified them. Thus, sorting out your folder, making a list of things to do, tidying your desk, phoning a friend to clarify a point or photocopying some notes you need can occupy the low-energy points, whilst creative tasks like writing, problem-solving or designing can occupy high-energy times.

8. Use people in the right way
If you have made the best use of people to help you prepare to do the part of the study task you are now tackling, you will be happy to work on it by yourself. However, if you feel that you would still like to clarify some aspect of the task or gather some more information from a tutor or friend, then that becomes your first study task. It means you are ready to study by picking their brains (which is part of an effective approach to coursework).

Motivating yourself
There are a number of ideas you can use to improve (or even find any!) motivation:

- Talk about what you are worried about with friends or an objective outsider such as a tutor or counsellor.

- Remind yourself of what you are doing 'it' (the study task) for, keeping your dream and goals in mind.

- Picture yourself doing it well and enjoying it.

- Pin sheets of paper on the wall.

- You can pin up A4 sheets of paper in front of you as reminders.

- When you are flagging or unmotivated you can look up and remind yourself of what you are doing. It helps keep you focused on an assignment, a revision topic or why you are bothering to study at all.

I WANT TO BECOME A P.E. TEACHER	**HOW HAVE LEISURE PURSUITS CHANGED IN BRITAIN SINCE 1945?**
i.e., *Why* are you studying	i.e., *What* you are doing e.g., the assignment question the revision question

- Get away from it purposefully – not to escape because you are avoiding tackling tasks – but because you know you need to do something entirely different so as to come fresh to a task.

- Remind yourself of a feeling of well-being or good achievement you had in the past. Go inside yourself and picture what you were like, how it felt – the total sensation of that moment. You can use the feeling of well-being to tackle current revision tasks. You can also picture the future, imagining yourself successfully completing tasks and enjoying the feeling of accomplishment.

- Think and talk positively. Avoid saying to yourself, 'I must get down to it' (a common phrase). See also **Talking positively** below.

- Use your best times of day to study (see page 37).

- Find and use the best place to study – one which 'feels' right and try also to find an alternative, second best, place (see page 27).

- Be imaginative in the type, variety and frequency of the rewards you offer yourself.

Talking positively

As you look at the two columns of phrases listed opposite, spot the words you say to yourself when you are tackling any coursework assignment or deadline. Circle the words you use most often.

I want	I must
I like to	I should
I will	I ought
I need to	I have to
I am interested in	They told me to
I am going to . . .	I was told I must . . .
I will do (task) by (when)	

If you find yourself circling some words on the right-hand column, see if you can shift yourself to words in the left-hand column; for on the left are the words that are more likely to motivate you and enable you to complete tasks. The words on the right are emotionally value-laden and oppressive in feel; they are less help in motivating yourself.

Being kind to yourself

Most of all, to motivate yourself, be kind to yourself. When people say 'Do you think I should push myself harder?' or 'I get tough with myself' or 'I force myself to do it', I often want to ask: 'Are you sure that is the way to motivate yourself?' Sometimes the answer is 'Yes, it is'. In which case, if you really know yourself well, that is fine. However, most of us will not sustain our motivation to study over a period of time by continuously being hard on ourselves or by forcing and pushing. The answer to many study tasks is not to beat yourself up for failing to do things but to reward yourself for doing something positive and constructively – however little the task. Thus it is helpful to treat yourself kindly or 'softly and gently' by:

- relaxing into what you are doing
- listening to music that aids your concentration (do not fool yourself on this)
- enjoying the rewards
- looking forward to whatever it is you are going to do
- enjoying the time, place and atmosphere to the full
- seeing time off, fun, sport and exercise, social life and time outside of study tasks as part of effective study, part of the balance of life.

Getting the balance right

If you get the *balance* right, you will be more energised for the study tasks. The people of Trinidad and Tobago have the verb 'to lime'. If you are 'liming' you are doing nothing much: hanging around with friends; having something to eat and drink; sunbathing; taking things easy. Talking to 1,300 fourteen to eighteen-year-olds in these two Caribbean islands, it was clear that the most successful students had the ability to both work and play, or were successful at study because they knew how to use the ideas in **Being kind to yourself** (page 25).

You can try to deceive yourself or deliberately lie to yourself about whether you are getting the correct balance between work and play. It is my belief that you will know when you are fooling yourself. You can get it wrong by overworking or overplaying but one thing is clear to me from the experiences of tens of thousands of students I have spoken to on this issue – *time away from tackling coursework assignments or revision is part of effective studying, not a separation from it.*

Finding it difficult to sustain your energy?

Even when you are tackling study tasks at your best times of day you may still find it difficult to sustain your energy. You can try the ideas in **Improving your concentration** (below) to maximise the use of the energy you have.

Improving your concentration

Improving concentration and your energy level is frequently *either* a matter of using more effective study approaches *or* resolving a personal concern which is interfering with your study. In the latter case, talking to someone may help, e.g. a friend, a relative, a teacher, doctor or counsellor, as described in **Using Others as Helpers** (Chapter 7).

The following study approaches will aid your concentration:

Finding a place to work
Find a place that has enough light, heat and space around for your books and papers. It should have a good feel to it – a place you like to be.

Assembling all the materials you need
Have all the materials you need assembled around you from the start: don't give yourself an excuse to postpone starting.

Devising questions
Devise questions to which you seek answers, as described in **Asking questions (page 12).**

Being active in what you do
You can be active by speaking aloud, taping answers on audio-tape, typing a list on the computer, talking to someone, writing notes and by using many other approaches in this book.

Choosing topics to study at which you are likely to succeed
Choose those of which you already:

- have some understanding
- find most easy to tackle
- have most interest in
- find useful
- know are most urgent.

You can find more specific ideas on how to do this in **Choosing what to revise** (page 49).

Setting yourself realistically small targets
This will give you more chance to succeed in reaching your goal. Success will increase both your self-confidence and your work rate.

Varying
Both the topics you study and the methods you use.

Studying for short periods of time, at least initially
15, 20, 25 and 30 minutes can be very effectively used on routine study. Short breaks can be used constructively either for relaxation or for recalling what you have been doing.

Resting and relaxing
Be positive about your breaks from study. Give yourself a day off a week at least and other free time when you are not obliged to feel guilty. A drink or a favourite television programme can be used as a reward for the completion of a specific study unit. Physical exercise, e.g. a walk, a run, a swim, yoga exercises or team games can help revitalise you, much studying is relatively passive.
    'I try to put aside an hour a day for myself, except when I am busy, when I put aside two.' (Ghandi)

Checking your sleep
Lack of concentration is often due to failing to look after a basic need for sleep. **Getting to sleep at night** (page 142) offers several ideas to help those with this difficulty.

CHOOSING WHERE TO STUDY

Where do you like to do your coursework? You can use this checklist to help you locate your best place of study – but notice some tasks are better performed in some places than others.

Checklist

- *Which rooms or spaces suit me best? e.g.* Bedroom, kitchen/dining room, study, lounge, library, classroom?

- *Where do I feel most comfortable? e.g.* Sitting upright at a table or an armchair? Lying on the floor or bed?

- *What rewards do I give myself?* e.g. Special food and drink, TV programmes, going out and meeting friends?

- *What atmosphere do I need?* e.g. An open window; a very warm room; a desk lamp, fluorescent light; natural daylight?

- *What sound do I need?* e.g. Complete silence; some background music or sound; headphones; types of music?

- *What do I need in my surroundings?* e.g. Books and papers assembled around me; a clear desk; papers on shelves nearby; TV on or off?

- *Do I need a specific view?* e.g. View out of window; posters or pictures; pinboard or noticeboard near desk?

- *Do I need people around me?* e.g. Someone in the home; work with another person (who?); best by myself?

- *Can I study outside – in all seasons?* e.g. Can I study in a car, on a walk or sitting by a stream or sea in any season of the year?

Picking the best environment

1. The key feature of where to study is that you seek for yourself a place where you like to be and where it is easiest to work. It must have a good feel to it: a kitchen table (where I am writing now); lying on your bed; at a desk, in an armchair, can all have this feel.

2. It is advisable to work some of the time at a desk, to prepare yourself for exam conditions, particularly closer to the exams.

3. A clear desk or table top, with enough space to have materials assembled and accessible around you. This will reduce time wasting and delaying tactics!

4. Your area of a room should be well lit (a table lamp may help), well ventilated and warm enough to be comfortable without causing you

to feel drowsy. It should also ensure you have the minimum unwanted interruptions and distractions.

5. A pleasant, non-distracting view can aid concentration. As I write I have a wall in front of me. It is light coloured and I can see two pictures I like and a chart on which I am ticking off my progress in writing this book. A pin board or wall chart in front of you can be very useful to plan and record your progress.

6. There is a lot of debate and argument in homes about whether you need to be working in a quiet environment. There is no single answer to this issue. If you, as the student, feel the need for quiet then it is important. If, on the other hand, listening to the radio, tapes or CDs aids your work, then continue to do so.

   Television is another dimension, for the visual image is powerful and watching television requires the use of two major senses. I can only listen to television when I am working, not watch and listen. Both can be used to advantage, by helping you relax and/or associating some sound or vision with a particular revision topic.

The essential point is to be honest with yourself. Is the environment you've created really helping your study – or acting, to some degree at least, as a substitute for studying?

ORGANISING STORAGE SPACE

I know from my own experience that so much time is wasted if I do not know where to find some notes I need to work on. It is not just time that is wasted, it is nervous energy too. I am often anxious about whether I am going to find what I am looking for; it delays getting started on the study task and I often have a sense of unease (a sort of mental unpreparedness) if I do not know where things are to be found.

Thus a place or places where you can leave your notes and books is an essential aid to completing coursework assignments for deadlines.

If you have not got such a place, ask for and negotiate some space in your home where you can leave things *undisturbed*; having to scoop up all your papers into a mixed up pile again is one of the particular time wasters.

If you are unable to leave things undisturbed on a table or desk then a bookcase or wall shelf is equally helpful. Alternatively you could keep subjects in a particular place in a room or rooms, thus psychologically separating out subjects.

Sometimes a filing cabinet, drawer or portable file can be obtained for this purpose. You can use file dividers to separate subjects and topics. It is beneficial to store files in chronological order of coursework deadlines and, in particular, to keep on hand the material relevant to your current work.

Whichever filing system you devise, it is important to keep an *index* or *catalogue* of what you have got where. It can be as simple as a sheet or two of A4 paper at the front of a ringbinder; it may be a simple card index; or you may choose to design a more elaborate system utilising the latest in technological innovation on a computer.

Colour coding your rooms, areas of work, files and file dividers to match your material to its relevant location in your system is also useful, e.g. the yellow area is English, the red is maths.

Whichever indexing system you implement, it will help you to remind yourself where to put things and to find them again.

In particular it will enable you to store, retrieve and resume tackling your current work with no wasted time or energy.

Keeping on top of your folders and portfolios

Typically, folders contain the raw material of your studies over a relatively short period of time. In portfolios you put your processed material, reviewed and refined, i.e. completed units, essays, assignments, reports, drawings, laboratory results, fieldwork notes, and all the other tasks you have completed over a year or two. Portfolios form the basis for assessment of your achievements over a complete unit, several units or an entire course.

Folders can become a mess, portfolios unwieldy. You may be tempted to stuff all your work into a folder or portfolio and then forget about it. To avoid last minute panic before examinations and/or assessments, you can reorganise your work periodically by:

- keeping it in order in plastic envelopes, when appropriate, to keep it undamaged and clean

- keeping it in a safe place, where it will not get lost or dog-eared

- rewriting illegible material

- rechecking and refining out-of-date material

- reviewing the material in your folders and portfolios, i.e. checking your understanding by asking yourself questions about it.

Building up regular reviews of your work is a key principle in learning that will make your final revision easier when you have developed the habit.

Starting a learning journal

This is a type of diary in which you can reflect on your learning, regularly, in short bursts. The format of your learning journal can be a book, a loose-leaf folder, a word processing file, audio-tape or video recording. Selected for your own ease and flexibility of use and accessibility, you can apply your learning journal to a variety of purposes:

- to make a list of things to be done

- to ask yourself, 'What – if anything – did I learn today?'

- to recall and capture something you have just seen, heard and understood today

- to help build your confidence in what you now know or have just understood properly, perhaps for the first time

- to list words that you want to look up in a dictionary or thesaurus to check their meaning

- to list questions that are still unanswered that you want answered

- to moan to yourself about those things that frustrate, confuse or worry you

- to connect something you have been doing on your course with something that has happened outside such as:
  – a conversation with a friend
  – an item in the news or on a TV programme
  – an article in a magazine

- to write or dictate a letter to an imaginary or real friend which explains your ideas and thoughts or lists your questions about a topic

- to comment on how you feel your contributions to your group were received

- to record the times of day and places you studied and reflect on how well it went

- to give yourself a pat-on-the-back for achievements, using it to encourage yourself.

Your journal can help you spot a pattern of effective study times more easily. **Tracking your time with a time chart** (pages 37–38) can also help you identify your best times for study.

Overall it can be an enjoyable task to keep a journal; it need not take up much time on a daily or weekly basis, although sometimes it will feel an effort to write in it. Overall a journal need not take more than ten minutes a day and it will be enjoyable to do.

Example
John, an American student used a journal: 'This was my first experience of writing a journal and I have to admit I did not care for the idea at all. As our course progressed, I found journal-keeping less of a chore and decided that there are some definite advantages. Because I was always on the alert for "suitable journal materials" I found myself thinking about different ideas, even when I was not studying them in class. It is a good rehearsal for a written exam, an opportunity to express myself through the written word. If a favourite topic of mine is not covered in an exam, I can write about it in my journal. Alright, I will admit it – keeping a journal can be enjoyable.'

Starting larger projects and dissertation
Typically, you will have months to complete, for example, a GCSE Design or History project, one unit of an S/NVQ or one first degree module.

If you are undertaking a course or programme of study which includes a larger project, a dissertation for your degree or several units which make up a whole qualification, your work can be spread over a longer period of time. For example, you may be given a complete year for a GCSE project, a dissertation is usually undertaken during the final year of a first degree and you may have up to three years to complete several units towards a full S/NVQ.

Sustaining your motivation over these longer periods of time brings its own special problems. Often you will have the larger project, the whole dissertation or complete S/NVQ in the back of your mind even when you are not working actively on it. You may find yourself ignoring it completely or haunted by the worry of it. You may also have a plan to work on this longer piece of work once you have completed other (shorter) coursework.

In general it is better to start on any assignment but especially a larger piece of work as early as possible even if it is in the smallest and simplest of ways. On a larger piece of work the following hints may be useful to keep your motivation alive.

KEEPING YOUR MOTIVATION ALIVE

You can keep your motivation alive by:

- Being clear about what you are being asked: checking the project title; keeping the question in mind; checking (or double-checking) what it means. If you are deciding the title yourself, spend active time getting it clear by talking it through with others. Check that your title is specific enough; ask yourself if you have enough sources of material for reference; and, most importantly, check that your title is exactly what you want to be working on.

• Breaking down the larger project or dissertation into small parts and tackling each in turn, thus achieving successful outcomes in a step-by-step manner.

• Studying in short but frequent bursts; doing a little – but often. It is never too late to start doing so, even if you have postponed starting for some time.

• Keeping track of what you are doing; your notebook or journal can help you process as well as record your progress. Exploring difficulties and juggling ideas will help you overcome problems without necessitating an ultimate 'best solution'.

• Using your tutor(s) as fully as possible. Once you have given the topic some thought and providing you are not seeking their advice too early nor expecting them to make decisions for you, your tutor is likely to be pleased to discuss your uncertainties with you. Giving prior thought and attention to the topic so that you have questions ready to ask them will ensure you use the time most effectively.

• Using friends and others to help you by (a) not expecting to do everything yourself and (b) talking aloud about problems with coursework or other issues that concern you. Revitalise your interest in the current subject or topic by talking to others and working together on aspects of your assignments.

• Knowing the question before you start; not wasting time on worrying or using up time on a task that has not been set; knowing exactly what you have to do. See also **Asking questions** (page 12) and **Using this approach for assignment questions** (page 15).

• Checking the regulations: knowing the minimum number of words per piece of coursework; counting the words (easy if you are using a computer) and sticking to the limits. If you have more words than needed, checking with a tutor whether this is likely to be penalised.

Using Post-its

Post-its are small pieces of paper that have a sticky edge which sticks to other pieces of paper. You can buy them in stationery shops throughout the world. Post-its come in different sizes and can be used for different purposes. Here are the three common sizes and some ideas on how to use Post-its.

52mm x 38mm (2 x 1½ inches)
- noting page numbers
- reminding you of what you want to do with this book or set of notes
- cross referencing, e.g. 'See Sociology notes too'

76mm x 76mm (3 x 3 inches)
- useful quotes
- a small cross-sectional diagram
- a small spider diagram
- a note to yourself

128mm x 76mm (5 x 3 inches)
- key points you want to include in an assignment reordered on a sheet of A4 or A3 paper to plan a structure
- memory joggers for revision
- lists of things to do today
- the names/dates/events you want to remember
- separate formulae you want to remember and apply

You can get them in different colours – yellow, green, blue, pink and even white, so you can colour code your work, too.

Using colour codes

You will probably find that you underuse colour to help you find the notes and subjects you are seeking. You can do this more easily by keeping study tasks and subjects in different coloured files such as:

- colour-coded sections in a ring binder
- coloured cardboard or plastic wallet envelopes
- see-through plastic envelopes with coloured zip-fasteners
- clear see-through plastic wallets in different tints.

You can also use

- coloured pens to put a clear indication on the top of pages on the same topic

- stars ★, triangles ▽, squares □ and dots ● in different colours to indicate grouped material. You can buy these stick-on shapes both with wall-planners and from big stationery stores.

Using colour in reading

Most of what we read is black lettering on white background, like this book. Most of what we write in ink is black or blue on a white background. It is not the easiest colour combination to read; for those with certain dyslexic conditions the contrast between black and white appears to make print jump or blur.

Some dyslexic students minimise the problem of reading their printouts by printing out their work from the computer onto coloured sheets – pale green, blue, grey and yellow. In the past, some have used coloured acetate sheets in pink, yellow, blue or green hues to lay over print as they read. A few have used specially prepared and purchased colour-tinted spectacles to minimise their difficulties with reading.

Nowadays, computer technology allows the user to change the default settings of both screen and text on a computer across a broad spectrum of colours to suit themselves. If you don't know how to do this, a friend, a peer or a tutor may be able to help you.

Using different colours for writing papers help you to:

- find some topics more easily in your piles of notes by this colour coding

- break up the uniformity of white sheets of paper to make things readable

- vary your use of blue, yellow, black and white in written notes to ensure you are using the most readable colours

- add Post-its in yellow, white or blue to sheets of other coloured paper to break up the sameness of colour.

Using a photograph album

You can make use of a flip-over plastic-sleeved photo album for keeping key word cards that you are using for an assignment such as an essay, a talk or a piece of revision. Cards can be arranged in the appropriate sequence to enable you to remember them; they can also be seen clearly and not get mis-ordered or damaged.

You can follow the story-line of a talk easily by flipping over the cards or use question-and-answer cards to enable you clearly to make links and associations between ideas. If you decide to change the order in which the information is arranged, the cards can easily be rearranged or slipped out and stored elsewhere, with a fresh topic replacing the one you were studying.

Completing the task – the idea of Gestalt

Gestalt is a German word for which the closest translation in English is 'completing the whole'. Once you grasp the idea, it can be enormously helpful in removing the day-to-day tension of study.

What it means is that you plan study so that you finish a particular task without leaving a part of it undone. These can be small tasks such as making outline notes on a question, organising a pile of notes or writing a first outline of an introduction to an assignment.

What you are aiming to do is to experience a feeling of completion, a feeling that you have done as much as you are able to do at one attempt. If you have judged it right and completed the gestalt, you can walk away from a study task without feeling anxious or burdened but with a feeling of having properly put the task down – no matter how small it was.

KEEPING TRACK OF TIME

You can keep track of time in a number of ways. *On a longer timescale* you can monitor the year, the term, the month or the semester (which is increasingly common in higher education).

You can either buy a 12-month year planner, available in an academic year version as well as a calendar year version, or you can make your own with poster paper or a series of A4 sheets. On them you can mark:

- deadlines for submission of assignments

- dates you were given assignments and dates for their completion

- the length of time you have for a particular assignment or project.

Using separate coloured lines to indicate the total number of days or weeks you have available to complete them, you can see at a glance when you have several deadlines occurring around the same time. You will also be able to identify visually the amount of time you have available for any project and spread your energies between them. This is known as a GANNT chart.

On a weekly basis you can fill in a timescale such as that in Figure 2 to monitor how you actually use time and to spot the most useful and usable times of the week for coursework tasks. There is another version of a weekly time chart usable during revision times on page 62, which divides the week into 21 sessions.

On a daily basis give some thought to trying to spot your best times to tackle the various tasks of study – and the times to relax, play or catch up with chores.

Tracking your time with a time chart

If you have difficulty in making time for study or in finding a balance between revision and other activities, completing the time chart (Figure 2) may help you identify the most useful times to tackle various study tasks.

How to use the time chart

- Fill in the spaces in the daily record at the end of each day, indicating what you did in each period of an hour or half-an-hour. Record what you did, not what you intended to do.

- Use highlighting pens to indicate the most frequently usable times for study.

- Draw up a new timetable which indicates your best times for study each week. If you can spot two or three hours on five days a week, you will have the basis of some study time to use each week.

Deciding on your best time of day – and your second best

If you know something about when you study most effectively you can choose to concentrate your energies on those tasks which are best tackled at particular times of day.

These are times you can best use for writing, tackling tricky problems, or giving some time to **Brainstorming** ideas to yourself (see page 172 for how to use brainstorming with others).

There are some times that you can routinely ignore for study purposes either because of tiredness or because experience tells you they are best spent doing other things – cooking, watching television, going for a walk, making phone calls, listening to music, having a swim, meeting a friend, tackling some chores or giving time to someone who needs it.

In this way you can, with practice, give yourself guilt-free, unhaunted time off.

Managing second-best times

There will be plenty of times when you feel stuck in a particular place at a particular time and know that the time could simply be wasted. Although there may be real advantages in spending the time having a chat with a friend or going for a drink, there are many things you can do which fit into these potentially wasteful hours. Here are some examples:

- Jot down ideas or tasks on Post-its.

- File paper away into the correct place in your filing system.

HOURS	MON	TUES	WED	THURS	FRI	SAT	SUN
a.m. 12-5							
5-6							
6-7							
7-8							
8-9							
9-10							
10-11							
11-12							
p.m.12 -1							
1-2							
2-3							
3-4							
4-5							
5-6							
6-7							
7-8							
8-9							
9-10							
10-11							
11-12							

Note: If you are attending full-time education during the day, you may find it more useful to record half-hour units in the late afternoon and evening, as well as in free time and lunch-times during the day.

Fig. 2. A time chart.

- Check your diary to spot other useful times ahead.

- Sort out materials needed for the evening or the next day.

- Photocopy a handout.

- Talk to a friend by telephone about a particular study task.

- Discuss a study problem with a friend over a coffee or cold drink.

- Look up a book in the library.

- Rewrite a review or revision card.

- Copy up some missing notes from a friend.

- Edit a piece of text.

If only some of these ideas fit into your second-best time spaces, what other ideas would you have to make better use of the time and place? Jot down any creative ideas you have – and keep alert to other creative ways of using these less than ideal times.

Saving time
Your can also save time if you:

- Colour code your notes in plastic or cardboard envelopes so you know where to find them at a glance.

- Put a marker in a book to indicate where you will need to start reading. You can use a bookmark, a card or a Post-it note (which will stick on) for this purpose, writing notes on it to remind you what questions you want to answer or which pages are relevant.

- Make the best use of computers. Type in ideas when you get them, saving them for later retrieval. Index work for ease of retrieval, listing tasks and deadlines to remind yourself what to do when, then cutting and pasting into an appropriate place.

- Do a little each day on tasks you feel are long-term or difficult to handle. Little and often is the rule and spending 10 minutes for five or six days in a week will soon enable you to see progress on a bigger task like a project or dissertation. For very specific study tasks you can successfully use very short periods of time such as 2, 5, 8, 10, 12, 20, 25, 30 or 40 minutes for:
  – arranging piles of paper in the correct order
  – jotting down questions you want to use when reading a particular book
  – recalling the five key points you have just read by writing them on a card

– drawing a diagram or cross-section
– sketching the first ideas on an assignment
– creating a spider diagram of your first ideas
– calling a friend to check your understanding of a question
and many more such tasks.

Changing time patterns?
If you change your routine, for whatever reason, this pattern may alter in such a way that previously unusable times become usable.

If your normal pattern changes during busy periods when you are completing assignments or preparing for an exam then try out a new time for routine tasks or creative ones.

You may also be forced to use routine times for more creative tasks because of pressure. If you have to do so, sometimes you can find yourself in a groove which enables you to be more creative than usual; you may reap the benefit of sustaining focus on a task.

Meeting deadlines
This chapter is filled with ideas for meeting coursework deadlines and in the rest of the book you will find ideas for meeting revision deadlines for exams too. However, there are some guidelines which can be applied to all tasks you face.

Starting something early
If you write something down, even if it is only a few ideas on a scrap of paper, you feel as though you have made a start. As long as you are careful to put the piece of paper away in a file or folder where you can find it (see page 29), you will gradually accumulate the tasks you have completed. It is beneficial to do something immediately you have been given an assignment. This is the principle used in writing this book; I have collected useful ideas in a series of files so that every time I have gone to write something, there is something to start on.

Creating an outline
Do some outline plans of what it is you are going to write or design. Allow yourself several attempts; do not feel you have to 'get it right' at a first attempt. Freeing yourself from believing that you have 'got it right' immediately enables you to explore new ideas without stagnating.

Making a rough draft
When you have enough material, try a first very rough draft of your final piece of work. Even in stages, a draft introduction or a draft of the middle section, will save you time and improve the quality of the final

version if you get the drafting stage right. You can redraft your first rough outlines, until you are satisfied.

Using school or college time to the full
You can make a start on many course tasks before you go to your home. By finding some information from a library, working quietly in an empty classroom or by talking to a friend about the task you have to do you can save time you would otherwise spend at home.

Having a Cosmo hour – or day
Magazines like *Cosmopolitan* are packed with articles which contain tips on how to overcome problems – of all kinds. One student came up with the idea of a 'Cosmo day' when they would pick up one of the self-improving ideas in such articles and apply it to themselves. One such idea is to allocate one hour, one morning/afternoon or day to doing the task you had not been doing – the one you had been putting off.

You can decide that the hour has arrived when you are going to tackle the task and positively set about it – no more running away from it in your frightened state. In this sense, it involves the saying:

Feel the fear and do it anyway.

USING COMPUTERS TO HELP WITH YOUR STUDIES

Schools, colleges, universities and many workplaces now are thronged with students undertaking academic or vocational qualifications who are making excellent use of computers to facilitate their studies.

If you have the advantage of access to a computer and are attracted to making use of it for your studies, there is a wide range of facilities you can draw on to tackle coursework and deadlines. You can check out your own use of one in **Using a computer – a checklist** on page 42.

Do you have to use a computer to do your coursework?
How much use you will be able to make of a computer will depend on the amount of time you have access to one. You will have more scope to draw on its facilities fully and creatively if you have your own to use whenever you need it, as opposed to the use of a school, college or workplace computer for a few hours a week, in competition with others.

The range of facilities available to you will depend on the sophistication of the hardware (the computer itself) and the software (the programs that can be run on it). While hardware and software are becoming ever more sophisticated in the range of facilities they offer, they are also increasingly user-friendly.

Whatever course you are studying, at whatever level, it has become accepted that you will need to develop some familiarity with computers during your studies. In particular, many students find word processing packages, spreadsheets, database and desktop publishing applications invaluable for entering and manipulating text, numeric data and graphics, to produce and present portfolios, essays, projects, reports, and dissertations of a very high standard.

Although you can still in Britain and other countries study for many qualifications, up to and including degree level, without any computing skills (by submitting handwritten essays or having your work typed up by someone else), it has become the norm that students develop at least word processing skills. There is little doubt that the trend towards widening computing proficiency will continue into the twenty-first century.

Moreover, there are some courses, both academic and vocational, which are difficult to complete or, at least, on which you are at a disadvantage without a computer of your own. One obvious example is if you are undertaking an Information Technology or Computer Programming course. In a subject like Electronic Engineering, you are highly disadvantaged in relation to your peers if you are not able to work on and present a final year project using your own equipment.

Using a computer – a checklist

Functions

Do you/could you use it this way?
✓ Yes   ? Perhaps   X No

- For keeping a database of resources

- To create a list of what you have so far completed – topic by topic

- As a notebook or journal to record your thoughts, feelings and ideas see **Starting a learning journal** (pages 31–32) see **Keeping a diary or notebook** (page 58)

- As a reminder pad or desk diary

- For entering the text of an assignment

- As a word processor and editor

- For 'number crunching' (i.e. sorting and analysing numerical data)

- To produce graphs and visually
  clear printouts, (i.e. striking and
  perhaps colourful)

- As a research tool (i.e. 'surfing the
  net' for information, ideas and
  perhaps inspiration)

- As an alternative medium for
  communicating with your family,
  friends and tutors (i.e. 'using e-mail')

- Other uses (specify...)

GETTING HELP IN USING COMPUTERS

Whether you are an absolute beginner or well practised in the use of computers, there is a wide range of specialist help available throughout the education system. Computer services in education may offer one-to-one advisory sessions, interviews, drop-in problem clinics, or open-access training sessions on the use of specific software such as word processing or spreadsheet packages.

If you prefer to help yourself on your own computer, there is an impressive range of interactive, computer-based training packages available commercially and through the Internet. You may be aware that most software packages available nowadays include their own 'step-by-step tutorials' to help you get started as well as comprehensive 'help' facilities within the program. It is well worth exploring some of the suggestions they offer.

Some people value and enjoy working with others. You can use friends and classmates to help each other. One group of four mature students spent a whole Saturday together (with a pub lunch in the middle of the day) and taught themselves a desktop publishing package, i.e. *Harvard Graphics*. Each of them was then able to use the program to enhance subsequent coursework.

'E-mailing' a friend about a problem or to ask a specific question can provide 'on-line help' almost immediately with the added bonus of 'live contact' with another person who may also have been struggling on alone.

There is much expertise around to be tapped amongst your friends and peer group of students; it is valuable and fun to share.

3
Organising Your Revision

REVIEWING AND REVISING

Misnaming revision
Much revision is misnamed – for three reasons:

1. You find yourself learning and memorising topics that you have not previously learnt. Although they are part of the syllabus and you may have taken notes on the topic, attended the course or received handouts, you gaze at the 'revision' material as if you have never seen it before.

2. You know you did not understand the topic at the time you met it in the study programme and realise that it is later, during your revision, that you attempt to understand it for the first time.

3. If you use the review-as-you-go techniques you will find you do not separate revision from the rest of your studies. It will mean you start revising from an early stage of your studies by constantly reviewing what you are doing. This will build up a collection of notes, cards and materials which you can use when it gets closer to your exams – the time usually described as the 'revision period'.

Reviewing
You will find examples of these reviewing techniques throughout Chapters 2, 3 and 4. They include:

- **Keeping on top of your folders and portfolios** (page 30).
- **Starting a learning journal** (pages 31–32).
- **Building up good revision notes** (pages 53–54).
- **Using notes with computers** (pages 54–55).
- **Using patterned notes** (pages 55–56).
- **Keeping a diary or notebook** (page 58).
- **Using a basic revision method** (pages 63–64).

CHECKLIST: YOUR REVISION PROBLEMS

I have/may have problems with	Tick if it applies to you	Brief Tips	Where to find out more (pages)
Getting started with revision		Make a list of what you have got to do subject by subject. Use the system suggested in this book.	47–50
Deciding when I should start revising		Now. It's never too early to start and you can revise until close to the exams.	44, 46
Understanding what I am revising		Ask yourself questions about what you are doing: know what you are revising and why.	12–16 46
Leaving my revision too late		Try doing a small piece of revision on a topic that interests you *now* – thirty minutes may be enough. Nibble away at the revision.	44 45 59–60
Revising by myself		Know what you are doing (see *Choosing what to revise*) Could you and a friend help each other?	49–50 168–169 171–173
Making a revision timetable that works		Have a trial period of a week or two to get it right. Be flexible.	58–61
Knowing the best way to revise		See *How to revise*. It is essential to recall what you have just tried to learn *immediately*.	61–64
How to use my notes and/or books for revision		Use your notes if you know they are good enough. Improve them and reorganise them if they are not.	53–56
The order in which to revise subjects or topics		See *Choosing what to revise* Vary subjects and topics to keep your interest going.	49–50
Knowing which topics to revise		See *Choosing what to revise* Know your strengths and weaknesses. Look at old exam papers. Speak to people who can guide you.	49–50
Revising mathematics and other number-based subjects		Practise answering questions without books giving you answers. Time yourself for exam length answers.	92–94
Whether to revise all topics or to ignore some		You can't usually revise all topics equally well. Most people like to cover at least 70%.	51–52
Concentrating		See *Improving your concentration*. Make sure you've got a good place to revise.	26–27
Making enough time for revision		Although there is never enough time and you need breaks, time off and relaxation, planning a revision timetable will help.	58–61 62
Finding a good place to revise		Find a place where you like to be and which has a good feel to it.	27–29
Deciding how many hours a day or week to revise		Make a weekly timetable. This can help decide the number of hours you revise. This will vary from 15 to 40 hours a week of private study. Set yourself daily targets.	58–61 62
Whether to take time off for relaxation and a social life		Take short breaks and at least a day a week and an evening or two off.	58–61 62

- **Using key word revision cards** (pages 64–68).
- **Testing yourself** (page 74).
- **Nine steps to a better memory** (page 75).
- **Reviewing over time** (pages 75–76).
- **Recalling a four-step system** (pages 76–77).

However, you may be looking at these ideas with a few days or weeks to go until your exams, without having reviewed your work regularly. The good news is that you can still learn a great deal by following some simple guidelines for effective revision.

You can apply these features of effective revision as you plan your revision tasks and organise your time.

Revising effectively

Effective revision replaces shallow learning with learning in some depth; replaces bewilderment with confidence; replaces the myth of a few fortunate people with photographic memories with the realisation that *you* too can use your visual memory to aid recall; and replaces the common – and useless – feeling of guilt with a structured revision programme.

The features of effective revision are that you:

- set yourself a *clear and specific target*

- *set a timescale* for each task, not 'I must do it', but 'I must do it by X time'

- pick *a task which is sufficiently demanding*, i.e. that is neither too easy nor too difficult at that moment

- can *verify your success* in learning the topic both to yourself (by testing yourself in some way) and to others (by using them as testers, for example)

- have a *feeling of accomplishment* after completing the task.

Once you have found your best places to study – see **Choosing where to study** (page 27) and **Picking the best environment** (pages 28–29) – then you have some decisions to make about how to be most efficient in:

- **Planning your revision** (pages 47–58)
- **Organising your revision time** (pages 58–61)
- and deciding **How to revise** (pages 61–70).

If you are not sure where to begin try the:

- **Checklist** on page 45.

PLANNING YOUR REVISION

1. *Developing a complete picture* of what you might be examined on in a particular subject will help you decide what to revise and with which topic to begin your revision. Using the suggestions below will prevent this from being overwhelming.

2. You can develop this whole picture by consulting *a syllabus* for the course. If you have, as is quite common, never seen one, your subject teacher is likely to have one and libraries in schools (sometimes) and colleges, polytechnics and universities (usually) keep copies. It may not be necessary to find the syllabus, however. Many internal examinations, i.e. exams set and marked within the school or college, are based upon the work you have actually been presented with during the year. Thus, the main topic and sub-topic headings from your notes or handouts from teachers and lecturers can give you quite a complete picture. Questions you have been answering and emphasis given to particular topics can give further guidelines.

   It is advisable that you check with teachers and lecturers about the scope of the examination (and use any guidelines you obtain from them).

3. You will find that anxiety you feel about 'covering the syllabus' is reduced if you are clear and specific about what you are revising, why you are revising it and how it fits into the overall revision of that subject. One way of deciding this is to *take a separate sheet of paper for each subject* you are studying and write on it the *principal topics* and *sub-topics* that you have studied on the course leading to the examination. For some subjects you may need a second sheet of paper. Arrange the topics and sub-topics in columns, allowing 4 or 6 cm space between each column.

   To clarify terminology in *Kate's example* (page 50) 'Geography' is the subject, 'National Parks' is the topic and 'Homes in National Parks' is a sub-topic.

Working with subjects, topics and symbols

Once you have listed the principal topics and sub-topics for each subject, you can use the simple symbol system in Figure 3 to indicate the amount of interest, understanding/knowledge, ease or difficulty, urgency and usefulness of each.

How much *INTEREST* do you have in it?		Very interested
		Quite interested
		A bit interested
		Not interested
How much *UNDERSTANDING AND KNOWLEDGE* do you have of it?	OKAY OK ? ??	Clearly know/understand it
		Know it/understand it quite well
		Understand/know a bit but probably not enough for *pass* answer standard
		Don't know it/understand it at all
How *EASY OR DIFFICULT* do you find it?	EASY EASY DIFF DIFF	Easy to do/understand
		Quite easy to do/understand
		Quite difficult to understand
		Most difficult to understand
How *SOON* is the exam: how much *TIME* do you have?	!!! !! !	Very soon; little time
		Soon, some time
		Quite soon; a bit more time
		Some way off; most time
How *USEFUL* is it? For example, how likely is it to come up in the exam? How useful is it for other topics or subjects? Can you use it in your everyday life?		Essential
		Useful
		Of some use
		Of no use
How much *CONFIDENCE* do you have in tackling this topic?		Very confident
		Quite confident
		A little confidence
		No confidence
How *RELAXED* are you about this topic?		Very relaxed and composed
		Quite composed
		A little anxious
		Uptight and panicky
How good is *ACCESS TO MATERIALS* you need?		Plenty of materials readily available
		Enough available to me
		Worryingly little material accessible
		Can't find a thing or can't get to it
How much *IMPORTANCE* is placed upon the topic or task by you and your tutors (if there is a difference – notice it)	IMP. IMP. IMP. IMP. IMP. IMP. UNIMP.	Of vital importance
		Quite a lot of importance placed on it
		Only a little importance
		Unimportant

Fig. 3. A simple symbol system.

Completing the symbol system

- You don't *have* to use a symbol from each of these five sections above. Thus, if *usefulness* does not seem relevant to a particular topic, then do not write that symbol next to it.

- You can invent your own symbols if you'd prefer; there's nothing magic about these.

Deciding priorities

Using the symbol system can help you decide your priorities. Look in particular for circled symbols, both positive and negative. *Circled positive symbols are a good starting point*, particularly if there are two or more together. This is particularly the case if you are finding it difficult to get started on your revision or your concentration has been poor. It will help your confidence to tackle a topic at which there is a high probability you will succeed. The second most positive symbol also represents topics that you are likely to be able to revise competently at an early stage.

You are probably going to find it more difficult to learn and immediately recall those *circled negative symbols*, particularly if you only have a short time left in which to revise.

Choosing what to revise – and in what order

Example

Kate, aged 15, has listed some principal topics on her Year 10 Geography syllabus. Next to each topic she has written symbols to reflect her *interest, understanding/knowledge* and the *ease or difficulty* she finds in each. Later she describes how she uses it to decide what to revise and in what order.

- You can mix in some topics with the more negative symbols in between those topics with more positive symbols, as your revision progresses and your confidence grows.

- Some people like to tackle some difficult topic first. They may feel by doing so that they have set themselves a positive challenge or challenged their fear. There is no correct order. Choose the order that meets your needs.

In the example, Kate said:

'I will start by revising the work which I found most difficult and the work which I did earlier in the course. I will do this because when I sit down ready to revise I am at my most alert and my concentration is good.

'By looking at the list I made for revising, I will mix in early topics I did, e.g. 'Types of Landscape', 'Granite Tors', with topics which I

Geography Revision

DARTMOOR

1. Types of Landscape ✓✓✓ OK (EASY)
2. Granite and Tors ✓✓✓ OK (EASY)
3. Landscape Weathering ✓✓ OK EASY
4. Relief and Temperature ✓ OK EASY
5. Dartmoor Traffic Flow ✓ OK EASY

National Parks
1. Position of all National Parks in UK ✓? EASY
2. Dartmoor as a National Park ✓✓ ? EASY
3. Homes in National Parks ✓? EASY
4. Conflicting Interests in National Parks ✓? EASY

Blackton Manor Farm
1. System farming on a farm ✓ OK EASY
2. Map of Uses on farm ✓? DIFF

PHYSICAL FACTORS IN FARMING
1. Systems ✓? EASY
2. Middlefell farm Langdale ✓✓? EASY
3. How do Soils affect farming ✓? EASY

Von Thünen
1. Cost of Transport ✓✓ OK EASY
2. Graphs ✓ OK EASY
3. Distance from farm Affect Land use ✓ OK EASY

Land use around a Town
1. Moncton ✓? EASY
2. Sampling Graphs ✓✓ OK EASY
3. Anomalies ✓✓ OK EASY
4. Scatter Diagrams ✓✓ OK EASY

Hill Farming
1. The Effect of Slope on Farming ✓? EASY
2. Income each Year ✓✓ OK EASY
3. Significance ✓? DIFF
4. Trelowseth Manor farm ✓? DIFF

Farmers Land Use Decision Making
1. Diagram ✓✓ OK EASY
2. Ability to see need for Change ✓✓ OK EASY
3. Reason for Farming ✓ OK EASY
4. Reasons for Farming ✓✓ OK (EASY)
5. A Herefordshire Farm ✓✓ OK EASY

Stages in the Development of Agriculture
1. Hunting and Gathering ✓✓ OK EASY
2. Subsistence Farming ✓✓ OK EASY
3. Peasant Farming ✓✓ OK EASY
4. Commercial Farming ✓✓ OK EASY
5. Major world Farming Patterns ✓? DIFF

found difficult, e.g. 'Significance of Hill Farming' and 'Major world farming patterns'.

'I will revise last the subjects I found easy, e.g. 'Reasons for Farming' and those that are fresh in my mind, e.g. 'Hunting and Gathering', 'Subsistence Farming'. I already understand these quite well and they will not take long to learn when I come to finishing off my revision.'

Kate's choice of order for topic revision feels correct to her. It is a subject in which she has a fair degree of confidence: a fact reflected by the large number of positive symbols on the page. This confidence enables her to start her revision with some relatively difficult topics. If the page had been covered with negative symbols, it would probably have been the best confidence-building plan to start with a few positive symbols.

Noting what you've revised – and completed

Example

Cathy used a white board she could wipe clean when she had completed tasks. She recorded all revision tasks on it and wiped off items as completed, every hour or two. At the end of the day she cleared it and started a fresh one for the next day. Thus progress was seen by tasks disappearing.

Encouraging revision of difficult topics

Example

Colin devised a system to revise for pharmacy degree final exams and gave this report on how it was progressing with about four weeks to go to the exams:

'In an attempt to cover the topics I had rather not, I used a system of ticks. An example – under Pharmaceutical Chemistry (Pharm Chem) I have covered the topics of:

1. Enzyme inhibitors
2. Anticancer drugs
3. Anti-inflammatory drugs
4. Optical isomerism
5. Anti-AIDS therapy
6. Prodrugs
7. Drug stability and interactions
8. Isoteric modification.

Firstly I cover the subjects I enjoy, and have a personal interest in, ticking them off as I go with my '*colour tick system*':

Red tick   = Read
Green tick = Revision notes made (in glorious Technicolor)
Blue tick   = Reread and flashcard written
Black tick = Exam question covered.

So the game is to read and make notes on the subjects in between and JOIN THE TICKS!! The contest is between Pharm Chem and the other four disciplines, to see which one will have the largest amount of continuous ticks.

(So far Pharmacognosy is leading with 7, then Pharm Chem and Pharmacology 5 each, then with Pharm Chem in a strong tactical position!!!)'

Spotting examination questions

Question spotting is a risky business. Given that an examiner could ask many different questions about a particular topic, trying to guess a particular question is obviously difficult. In many subjects a core of topics are going to appear, with some variation from year to year, e.g. a topic appearing in three or four years for a five-year period. In some examination papers there is some reasonably sure 'banker' question. Examinations which are set and marked *internally*, i.e. within the school or college, are going to concentrate on the actual topics which the teacher or lecturer has presented to groups during the course. It is likely that *topic spotting* is more reliable in these exams, whereas in *externally* set and marked examinations, e.g. most GCSE and Advanced level subjects, the emphasis of the questions will be to reflect the work of many students and their teachers. Different emphasis is likely to be given to topics in separate schools and colleges. GCSE includes internal and external assessment.

There is no substitute for extra work if you want to be certain of being able to answer the number of questions required. One effective way of preparing is to **Devise questions around a topic** (below), another to **List useful definitions** (below). The overall strategy is laid out in the flow diagram on page 53.

Devising questions around a topic

By practising asking questions about a particular topic you can increase your flexibility and preparedness for the examination itself. *List* past exam questions, grouping them into *types* of question and according to *emphasis* they may have in common. Add to these any questions you have been asked during your course and any that you and others could make up to give other angles on the topic. Check to see which questions occur most frequently on past papers, as one rough guide to the likelihood of particular questions occurring.

Example
Sylvia describes how she used old exam questions:

'Nearer exams I'd write an A5 sheet of past exam questions (you could buy some old exam papers from the Open University) on each topic and put the questions at the back of my A5 folder (see page 68) so I could also see them through the plastic by turning the folder over. Then, whilst walking to the shops or in any short break, I'd look at one question and think about what I would answer – if sitting down, doing a five-minute written plan.'

Listing useful definitions
Make lists of definitions of the *key words, ideas or concepts* that you

may need to use in the examination. Learn these as part of your revision. The following ideas can help you plan your revision.

Building up good revision notes
Organise and, if necessary, reorganise your notes by:

- Keeping all your notes, essays, reports and other material on a particular *topic* together. As the studying year proceeds it is often unnecessary for material to be separated because of the date you completed it or the type of material.

- Grouping related topics together for ease of revision: related topics can be revised together.

- Discussing your notes with others. Criticise them and, where appropriate, rewrite parts of them.

- Reducing your bulky notes to key words and key ideas as explained in **Key word revision cards** (pages 64–68). Use these cards for the major part of your revision, cross-referencing them with your original notes.

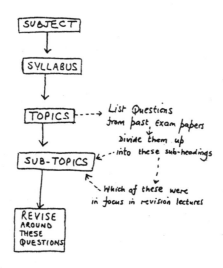

- Drawing together brief summaries of topics and sub-topics in a visually creative way. One method is to use simple *spider diagrams* as in Figure 4 to help you remember the main points of a topic. Each leg of the spider can be a different colour to help you differentiate between them, associating a colour and a piece of information. The number of legs your spider possesses will vary! These can be easily and quickly reproduced at the beginning of an exam.

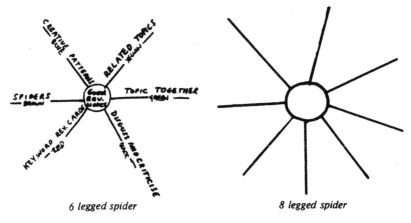

6 legged spider   *8 legged spider*

Fig. 4. Spider diagrams.

Using notes with computers

Example
Studying for a law degree, Kevin used this thorough system for revision and it helped him achieve an Upper Second.

1. He gathered all the papers together on one topic:

- notes on chapters from books
- photocopies of handouts or articles
- essays or assignments
- his own class/lecture notes.

2. He made key notes on all of the above, condensing the main facts and issues onto a few sides of A4 paper (3–6 sides).

3. He reviewed each side regularly, going over key facts several times in one session.
   Stages 1 to 3 he did from his handwritten notes.

4. He used a computer to list all the questions he could find on this (and every) topic. He made this into a quiz by typing questions onto the screen and then typing short answers to each.

In combining stages 1 to 3 with stage 4 he felt confident that he had a clear grounding in knowledge and that he was familiar with answering questions about it.

Using patterned notes

Patterned notes are another way of summarising your understanding and finding links and associations between information and ideas.

Usually when students make notes they try to force their ideas into a linear (straight line) structure, e.g.:

1. related topics
2. discuss and criticise
3. key word revision cards.

This often creates problems when they think of a new idea that does not fit into the structure. Alternatively, dissatisfaction with the order of the items, or remembering another item and having no space in which to add it can lead to several rewrites and reorderings.

Patterned notes help to overcome this problem. They can be used creatively to allow the mind to associate freely (they are sometimes called *creative brain patterns* or *mind maps*). They can also be used for summarising very quickly what you have just been revising. In five minutes, using this system, you can recall a complete topic on paper or card.

You start patterned notes in the centre of a sheet of paper. Your subsequent ideas can splay out around it. When you are using it creatively, don't attempt to evaluate your ideas, just write them down. When all your thoughts on the topic are down on paper then you can evaluate the ideas and decide which order you will put them in. By this method you are trying to separate the creative and evaluative processes of the mind. You can use colours to group information and ideas together and add numbers to indicate which ideas are most important or the order in which you would answer a question. Make your notes as brief as possible. They are just for you and don't have to make sense to anyone else.

Some best times to use patterned notes are: when you are about to start writing a piece of work, e.g. as an outline answer to a question in the examination; when you want to check your recall of the topic you have just revised; when you want to summarise some longer notes; in planning an essay or the answer to any coursework question; as a facing or front page to your more conventional notes, i.e. you can use the two forms of notes alongside each other. Experiment and find out when you find them most useful. More information about this approach can be found in Tony Buzan's book *Use Your Head*.

Using the patterned note approach – tips

1. Get a blank piece of paper and a pen or pencil. Sit somewhere you can concentrate for a few minutes.

2. Pick a topic that you know a lot about and in which you are very interested. It needs to be one where you'll have no difficulty having ideas, thoughts, facts and knowhow. It can be a hobby, a subject topic you know well or anything; it doesn't matter what.

3. Imagine you are trying to explain the topic to me and when you are ready, time yourself (or get someone to time you) for exactly four minutes to record, in your usual note-taking style, as many ideas as you can in the time. Time it exactly and stop writing the moment the time is up.

4. Now, using a fresh sheet of paper, time yourself to start again by putting your topic in the centre of the page and bringing out ideas from the centre; short key words or phrases spreading out from the centre. If you are uncertain where to place things, put them at the edges. Stop after exactly four minutes.

5. Compare the two. Are there any differences? Did you find one approach easier than the other? Did you get more ideas down in one rather than the other? If you tried this exercise with someone else, you can compare your notes and reactions.

Figure 5 is an example of a mind map to check whether you are ready to study.

Example
Jo immediately related to the idea of visualising a series of bubbles with ideas in them as an alternative to making a list or writing a paragraph of ideas. It is her natural way of seeing ideas.

Overviewing what you have to revise
Choosing what to revise – and in what order (page 49) offers suggestions on how to do this. This will help you decide how much to revise and in what order. How much of a subject to revise is a difficult issue. For the majority of examinations you can be very successful without

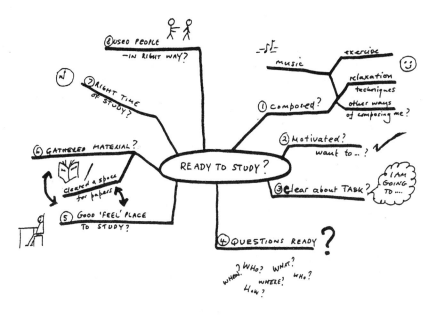

Fig. 5. A sample mind map.

attempting to revise 100 per cent of the syllabus. There are some examinations for some professional groups that demand very high levels of perfect knowledge about certain key areas, e.g. for doctors, accountants and lawyers. The majority of examinations and examiners do not expect the whole syllabus to be 'covered'. Obviously, the more you cover in your revision the more chances you have of finding questions you can answer. However, this will still depend on how carefully you have checked with your teachers, syllabus and examinations and which topics you have revised, e.g. it would be possible to miss a topic which is compulsory and worth more marks than other topics. **Knowing your examinations** (page 97) will maximise the chances of your finding questions you can answer.

My guess – and it is only a guess, with the provisos mentioned already – is that covering 70 per cent of a typical syllabus during revision would provide a good chance of finding enough questions to answer. As I consider this to be the least reliable guideline in this book, I would strongly recommend you seek the guidance of others, teachers and lecturers for each subject you take if you are concerned about this issue.

Keeping a diary or notebook

You can use a diary or notebook:

- To monitor your progress, commenting on how well you are progressing and noting points of which you wish to be reminded.

- To note down ideas and information as they occur. These can be transferred later to revision cards or notes.

- To plan the next day's work on the evening before.

- To keep by the side of your bed to note down good ideas, clear thoughts, information or even dreams that you have remembered. You can use it if you wake at night or first thing in the morning when you wake.

You may find other uses for them. You may also wish to carry blank postcards around with you for noting down the same sort of information, as an alternative or in addition to a diary or notebook.

Varying subjects, topics and methods throughout your revision

Vary these each week and each day. You will find that you are more likely to sustain your concentration by doing so. At the same time, mix the difficulty of the topics revised, using the confidence gained from one piece of work successfully completed to help you tackle a slightly more difficult topic.

ORGANISING YOUR REVISION TIME

Here are thirteen ideas to help you organise time:

1. *Make a revision timetable* going day-by-day from now until the examinations begin and for the period between examinations. The problem with revision timetables is that they often go wrong after the first day: to counteract this:

   – Have a two-week or one-week trial period to enable you to determine what tasks you can realistically complete in a day.
   – Be flexible, e.g. different subject headings for each day will enable you to vary the topics you revise.

   An example of a revision timetable is included in Figure 6.

2. *Pin up your timetable* or time plan on a wall in a prominent place, e.g. above your table or desk. Coloured pens can make it clear and attractive.

3. *Revise as you go:* start weeks before the exams. If you haven't started before reading this, start now. It's never too early to start and you can still revise until very close to your examinations. Starting six to eight weeks before the exam is a typical revision period for most students.

4. *Include in your revision* timetable any unfinished work you still have to do as part of your year's studies. You do not have to complete this work *before* starting revision. You can revise this subject work as soon as it is completed, so it can become part of your revision.

5. *Know how you use the one hundred and sixty-eight hours in the week.* You can use the **Time Chart** below to calculate exactly how you have used the time in one week and record hours in the various categories. Alternatively, you can do a rough calculation and complete the table below. You have been provided with a daily and weekly column; complete either or both according to which you find easier.

TIME CHART	Total hours	
	Daily	Weekly
Sleeping, dressing, washing, etc.		
Travel		
Classes, laboratories, etc.		
Going out socially		
Recreation and exercise		
Watching television		
Eating		
Domestic responsibilities and tasks		
Totals		
Hours remaining in the day/week that may be used for private study		
	(Total subtracted from 24 hrs.)	(Total subtracted from 168 hrs.)

6. *Set yourself a daily target of revision hours.* An alternative to a large-scale or weekly revision timetable is to set yourself a daily target of revision hours, e.g. four hours a day. This time unit can be shown on a chart marked off in quarter-hour units with your favourite colours, to show you effective and concentrated use of time. You could use this idea by itself or alongside marking off

topics you have revised on a chart.

Angela, a final year undergraduate, combined this with positive self statements ('It's really working', 'I've 40 whole days left') to successfully complete her revision. She monitored the quarter-hour units on a chart and felt a sense of achievement and optimism: there are a great many quarter-hours in four hours revision a day for 40 days!

7. *Working late at night.* As explained in **Getting to sleep at night** (pages 142–148) there are wide differences in people's ability to work effectively late at night or in the early hours of the morning. For a typical student three or four hours work in an evening is likely to be as much as they can effectively tackle. It would certainly not be advisable to work very late or long the night before an exam. On other nights, developing the effective self-monitoring this book is encouraging will enable you to decide whether you are working efficiently.

8. *For routine revision,* you can *work in short periods of time,* i.e. as short as 20–30 minutes. Some topics and subjects call for longer periods but numerous sub-topics can be revised in this way. Mathematical, scientific or problem-based revision will often require longer periods, e.g. one hour, to follow through a sequence of techniques and knowledge.

9. It is important to *set a time limit on completing a task,* i.e. 'I will do X by . . . '

10. *Reward yourself* by taking *breaks* of at least a few minutes between work spells. You can take longer breaks for a drink or to watch a favourite TV programme. Breaks can also be used for actively recalling what you have just been trying to learn.

11. *Divide the week into 21 sessions.* Another way of organising your time is to see the week as seven mornings, seven afternoons and seven evenings. Think of each session as a maximum of three hours long. Plan to work, formally in school or college or privately, around 15 sessions, giving a maximum working week of 45 hours, out of the 168 hours in the week. Using this system, ensure you take about six sessions for relaxation, entertainment and as a complete break from study.

Example
Katherine, aged 15, used this approach in the summer term before her GCSEs. She writes:

'My greatest problem in the past has been organising a successful work timetable – until! – I discovered your idea of dividing the day into three sessions, am, pm and evening. It REALLY WORKS! I have used it to plan all the work I have had this half-term.'

12. *The number of hours a week to revise* will vary widely according to the number of examinations you are studying for, how many subjects you are taking and the amount of formal study, *eg* classes, lectures you are continuing to attend. However, private revising time close to the examinations is likely to be a minimum of 15 hours a week and a maximum of around 40 hours a week if you are a full time student.

13. *A very important rule of thumb.* For every one unit of time, *eg* half an hour you give to reading, *ie* trying to take in or assimilate information, you should spend at least the same amount of time on trying to recall what you have just read.

   It is by recalling that we remember what we have read (heard or seen). So, the order is:

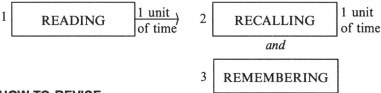

1 | READING | 1 unit of time ⟶ 2 | RECALLING | 1 unit of time

and

3 | REMEMBERING

HOW TO REVISE

In order to revise efficiently, you can draw upon a wide range of ideas about how we learn. These have been grouped together in Chapter 4 **Improving Your Memory** and are relevant to all subjects at whatever level. Additionally, specific ideas are included to help those studying mathematically based subjects, science and technology. In this section you will find a reliable **Basic revision method** (pages 63–64) and suggestions for **Using key word revision cards** (pages 64–68).

What is the commonest revision fault?
The commonest revision fault is to sit passively with book or notes open in front of you for hours, attempting to read and 'take it all in'. Frequently, the results are poor; you do not remember most of what you were reading; long periods are spent over the same page whilst feeling increasingly disheartened.

What method can you use to correct the fault?
The basic revision method (page 63) uses a number of different learning ideas in combination. It is very active; it involves repetition

The first week of this timetable is complete in some detail: other weeks can be completed in the same way. If you are continuing to attend full time education during the day, the evenings or weekends will become more important and can be sub-divided into smaller units, if necessary.

DAYS OF THE MONTH OF:	MON	TUES	WED	THURS	FRI	SAT	SUN
(Month)	7	8	9	10	11	12	13
a.m.	Subject A	Subject C	Voluntary work	Subject D	WHOLE DAY	Subject E	Subject E
p.m.	Walk Swann Coffee-friend	Shopping	Subjects B and C	Subjects B and C	VISIT TO	Review of ABCD	TV Friends home
Evening	Subject B (2 topics)	Subject A (1 topic)	Subject C	Subject B	TOWN	Meet friend at DISCO	Review cards Plan next week
	14	15	16	17	18	19	20
a.m.							
p.m.							
Evening							
	21	22	23	24	25	26	27
a.m.							
p.m.							
Evening							
	28	29	30	31	1	2	3
a.m.							
p.m.							
Evening							
	4	5	6	7	8	9	10
a.m.							
p.m.							
Evening							

Time already committed during the Examination and Revision period e.g. social events, classes, exams.

Time that may be available for revision: you would fill in subjects or topics in these spaces.

Fig. 6. A weekly time chart.

and testing yourself; it ensures you minimise mistakes; it involves using your visual and aural memory; it breaks down learning into manageable parts and ensures you are recalling recent learning.

If it is coupled with the **key word revision cards** idea (pages 64–68), you add to these concise, manageable summaries, colour and design to stimulate visual memory. Frequent use in very short bursts of time will ensure continued recall and retention of information.

Using a basic revision method

This is a basic method for most routine descriptive (word based) revision and some problem-solving, mathematical revision, involving either four or five steps.

Step one

Read your notes and seek answers to questions, as described in **Asking questions** (pages 12–15).

Be as active in your reading as possible, e.g. talk to yourself, walk around the room (even though people may give you funny looks). Speak into a tape recorder.

Step two

When you feel you have understood and can remember what you have read, close up your notes.

Step three

Now actively recall what you've just been reading, asking again the same questions without looking at your notes, until you have exhausted your recall of the whole topic you've been revising. Whilst doing so write down what you have recalled in brief notes on a card or a sheet of paper. It may help you to have the question written down to refer to in the recalling process.

Step four

Check the original notes with the new ones. Have you recalled all the answers to the questions you were asking?

If yes, you have created a *master card*, which you can use to re-revise without having to consult the original lengthier notes. *If no*,

Step five

Re-read your original notes as in Step one above, looking particularly for those points you originally missed. Repeat Steps two to four above, writing out all the points again, not just those missed the first time: by doing so, you will still be treating the topic as a whole and improving your recall of the whole topic.

This may appear time-consuming and cumbersome but it is not. It ensures a high degree of recall which reading a lot of notes does not do.

Using key word revision cards

Key word revision cards are a popular and effective way of developing your revision notes. The object is to write (or draw) brief outline notes immediately after you have completed work on a topic. Your intention is to record the minimum number of words to retain a full understanding of the information the next time you look at, and use, the card. These words – the *key* words – are designed to stimulate your recall of the topic without the necessity to write complete sentences or continuous prose. Cards can also be used for recording, and recalling, diagrammatic data, cross-sectional drawings, graphs, tables or formulae.

Starting your cards

You can start making these cards at any time, not just at those times, closer to exams, which you think of as revision times. Immediately you have completed a piece of homework or coursework you could summarise it onto a card, which as well as being a preparation for revision will become a part of revision. If you read an interesting article, see a relevant television programme or find a useful section in a book, brief outline notes on a card can quickly capture the moment.

The cards will quickly build up and can be grouped in subject/topic groups. They can be kept in boxes, plastic wallets and/or be held together with elastic bands.

Cards can be of any size. The three most popular sizes are A5, postcard size and a size somewhat smaller than postcard size. Postcard size tends to be the most popular as you can condense a considerable amount of information on to it and it is very convenient to carry in pocket or bag. Cards have advantages over paper in that they are more durable. A further advantage is that they help you develop confidence in your ability to manage the volume of revision you are required to tackle. Revising from a series of small, non-bulky cards seems so much more manageable than overwhelming piles of A4 notes in files or ring binders. You can always consult your main notes if a point on your card is unclear, amending your cards as you do so. Cards are easy to read on a bus, in a common room, waiting in a corridor or during a lunch-time or break from classes.

Advantages of using your own cards

There is nothing new about a card system like this. Commercially produced cards on particular subjects have become a growth industry over the last decade or two, e.g. 'Key Facts' cards and their rivals. Making your own can produce better notes for revision. This is because you can:

- Make them reflect your own understanding and knowledge; they are highly personal to you.

- Use space in a varied, interesting and more visually recallable way. Each card can be unique, making it very much easier to recall the information.

- You can use colour, boxes and underlining together with graphics, cartoons or diagrams to add vividness to each card. You could use a standardised colour system for your notes: black for information, blue for cross-referencing your own thoughts; green for headings; red for key names, dates, book titles. You can train yourself to recall both what you wrote and where it was located on the card. Associating the two will aid your recall of the card.

Some of the other useful aids are included in the outline of a revision card in Figure 7. Two completed cards, although reproduced without colour, give some idea of how to construct them.

Following Gail's card system
'Some people are able to revise from their lecture notes a few weeks, even days before the exam and do very well – great if you've got a photographic memory. Unfortunately, like many people, I have not, and need to learn the material and actively process it in a variety of ways.

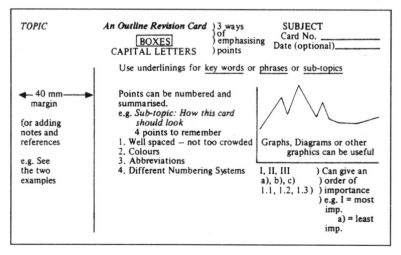

Fig. 7. An outline revision card.

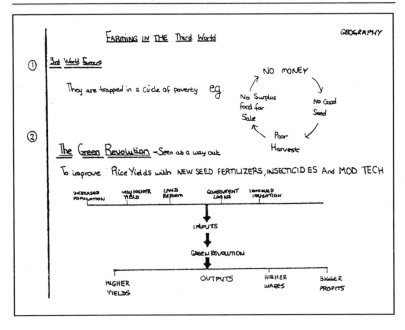

Example – Kate

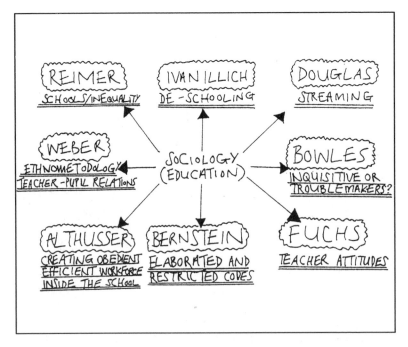

Example – John

Example – Gail

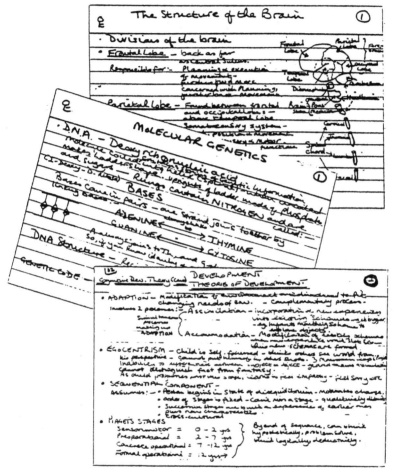

Some students rewrite the material onto A4 sheets, and I do find this practice very useful for integrating topics and summarising. However, for me the most effective way of deeply learning the wide breadth of topics was to rewrite the notes onto 6 x 4 index cards using fairly small writing and different coloured pens. I found that a sheet of A4 could be written onto one side and that in 2 card boxes I could store the whole year's lecture notes. This had a great psychological effect – enabling me to feel *in control*, and was also extremely practical as I could carry them virtually anywhere and revise in the most bizarre places.

'It is not a question of copying out lecture notes; instead it is necessary to actively process and condense them. This highlights any areas which aren't fully understood and enables problem areas to be addressed at this early stage rather than just before exams! Although time-consuming, this proved to be an extremely effective way to learn. An example is shown above.

'My early attempts were abysmal – I had previously tried using small index cards (4 x 3), putting single concepts on each card and filing them in alphabetical order. You may well see the foolhardiness of this notion already but I learnt the hard way. This was ineffective because my knowledge on specific concepts was completely disjointed and didn't permit any association with one another. I then realised that I needed to re-sort the cards, allocating them to various categories and thereby linking the information together. This was extremely laborious but taught me a very valuable lesson: the more I could integrate the pieces of information into a wider structure, the better I would be able to remember it. I set about producing a new set of cards.

'Other helpful methods are to read the notes aloud and also to tape them and play them back to yourself, perhaps in the car or whilst relaxing. I found that the more methods of absorbing information I could adopt, the better chance I had of actually remembering the material.'

Using A5 paper for revision notes
You don't have to use cards for your revision notes. Sylvia used A5 paper to revise for her Open University exams, which she found was a good system.

'I made notes on A5 paper and then, as I revised, gradually reduced my notes so that I could fit a whole topic on one side of A5 paper. I'd keep my longer notes of a topic in a plastic A5 holder (those like A4 ones which you can then put in a file) and keep all the plastic holders in a file – with dividers between sections, e.g. memory, language, perception and problem-solving when I was doing cognitive psychology.

When I reduced a topic to one side of A5, it became the sheet at the front and visible through the transparent plastic holder. I'd use different colours on that top sheet and write chunks in different parts of the sheet so I'd have a visual sense of what was written where on the page.

When I went anywhere within about six weeks of exams, one or several of these plastic folders went with me! So whenever I had a spare few minutes, e.g. waiting at a bus stop or during a coffee break at work, I could get one out and test myself. If I then found my top sheet wasn't full enough, I would have the more detailed notes underneath to check my knowledge with.'

Using TV and video

You can use TV programmes and video as part of your revision, particularly when you have collected relevant videos such as plays, documentaries and Open University programmes. Sylvia used OU programmes:

'I used to video all my OU programmes on TV then when I was near exam time but was too tired to keep revising, e.g. late evening, I'd watch one of the programmes. This meant I could relax a bit but also feel I was doing something useful and reinforcing what I was learning.'

Using abbreviations

You can use abbreviations to save space and time in either your revision cards or notes.

Three basic rules in using abbreviations
1. Be consistent in your use of your own abbreviations. Find a system and a set of standard abbreviations and stick to it.

2. Do not use abbreviations in work designed to be read by others, e.g. examiners. The exceptions to this are relatively few (e.g., i.e., *et al.*, viz. are most common).

3. Keep a note of your own common abbreviations, either in a notebook, on a card or at the front of your file.

In addition, you can devise your own abbreviations for the common terms used in the subjects you study. These would include:

– The subjects themselves, e.g. G = Geography; M.S. = Materials Science.
– The names of professions, e.g. Scs = Scientists; Ecs = Economists; Hs = Historians.
– Concepts, ideas, principles, common practices, e.g. c.w. = casework; Cht. = Chartism; strat. = stratification.
You can also abbreviate by:

– Leaving out unnecessary words thus keeping only the key words you need to understand what you have written, e.g. a, the. Shortening the ends of words, e.g. —ing becomes g.
– Leaving out syllables, e.g. transport becomes t'port.
– Using foreshortened versions of words you use frequently, e.g. cd = could; wd = would; shd = should; w/o = without.

This foreshortening is often achieved by leaving out vowels (aeiou). However, it is worth restating that you have to be consistent and use the abbreviations only one way, *eg* w/o = without in your abbreviation not 'won over' as it does in competitive sport.

Standard abbreviations

Some of the most common and useful abbreviations you can use in note-taking and key word revision cards.

p	= page	=	= equals, is the same as
pp/ps	= pages	≠	= does not equal, is different from
f	= following page		
ff	= following pages	<	= less than
ib, ibid	= *ibidem* = in the same book, chapter, passage, notes	>	= greater than
		∴	= therefore
e.g.	= *exampli gratia* = for example	∵	= because
op. cit.	= *opere citato* = in the work quoted	no.	= number
		qv.	= see
et al.	= *et alia* = and others	~	= about
viz.	= *videlicet* = namely	→	= it follows
i.e.	= *id est* = that is	alt	= alternative
cf	= *confero* = compare	fr	= from
c	= *circa* = about, approximately	exc	= except
v/vs	= *versus* = against	incl	= including
inf	= *infra* = below	opp	= opposite
NB	= *nota bene* = note well	neg	= negative
ref	= with reference to	pos	= positive
esp	= especially	usu	= usually

4
Improving Your Memory

LEARNING MORE ABOUT MEMORY

The 1990s have been the decade of research into the brain. It is clear that we are beginning to learn more about how the brain works, how we learn and remember and this chapter brings you some of those understandings and many practical ideas for improving your memory which are drawn from them.

Engaging the brain and senses

Here you will find ideas about how we can make use of both our left and right sides of the brain. Many students are being asked to engage in a number of left-brained tasks such as trying to be objective, rational, logical, theoretical and analytical in both writing and speech. This chapter is full of ideas for tackling these tasks by making the fullest use of your senses and thus bringing into use your right-brain characteristics such as the ability to visualise, be intuitive, draw ideas together and make patterns to help you with some of the left-brain dominated tasks.

You will also find ideas about the use of your eyes and your use of language in improving memory drawn from the field called NLP (neuro-linguistic programming).

You will find ideas for the active use of your senses in different combinations to enhance your memory and some ways of checking your preference for the use of your senses.

Improving your memory

The good news is that, whatever your age, your memory can be improved. To work well, your memory needs to be used often, be given its exercise, as it were. As you go through these memory ideas, pick out the ones you would like to try and notice the approaches you use most often. Try out different approaches until you find those that suit you. You can do this by seeing if they help you remember some items on a

CHECKLIST: YOUR MEMORY PROBLEMS

I have/may have problems with	Tick if it applies to you	Brief tips	Where to find out more (pages)
Improving my short-term memory		Try not to take in more than two or three pieces of information at most, at one time. Find links to what you already know.	75
Remembering formulae and mathematics		Do lots of worked examples tracing back to clear understandings. Use colour coding for formulae, adding visually absurd images to help recall.	81–83 92–94
Recalling the detail in diagrams and graphs		Use highly visual active technique, testing yourself on sections of the diagram. Use upward eye movements to aid visual recall.	81–83
Not remembering unless you revise close to the exams		Start immediately to make up brief question and answer cards (each unique and varied). Test yourself on the topic and do so again regularly for a few minutes. You will recall them.	74 75–76
Remembering what I have already revised		Review your key word cards or notes in short bursts at regular intervals by testing yourself.	64–68 74 75–76
No matter how hard you try you cannot remember what you want to remember		You are trying too hard – 'trying' is not a good idea; doing practical multi-sensory active things is a good idea.	77–78 79–91
How to remember dates and names		Big bold colourful drawings and images linking dates, events and people together.	85–88
Remembering facts		Pay full attention to the material in a relaxed frame of mind. Use your senses to the full to find links with the facts.	79–91
Your mind going blank when you know you know it		Understand how your eye movements affect recall; use it to help you unblock the memory. Start writing and doing something; learn some calming techniques.	75 85–87 126 139–140
Forgetting what you learned last week		Regularly review the topic at intervals suggested. Make sure you paid full attention to the topic by means of active techniques like Question and Answer.	12–14

shopping list or some phone numbers as well as using them to recall
something you are revising.

CHOOSING WAYS OF REMEMBERING

The best way of remembering is to have a real understanding of a topic
which has been achieved by finding the right questions to ask and
seeking answers to them. In this way, you come to see the connections
between things: how A links with B, B with C and so on.

Such understanding can be developed by some of the ideas that
follow, which will aid your recall of information.

Associating
Words, numbers or pictures take meaning in relation to the information
around them. It is these links with the information around them which
fundamentally affect their meaning.

A simple example would be the word LOVE. Its meaning and
context changes with the words around it. LOVE, Forty; the LOVE
bug; I LOVE you; God of LOVE – all conjure up very different
perspectives.

Where these links – these associations – form in chains, you may find
that a real and lasting understanding develops. Even if this fails to
happen, association techniques, both visual and verbal, can aid your
memory very effectively.

Grouping objects
Group items together and form links and associations between them in
your mind. You could practise this idea by the tray exercise, a well-
known game played at parties. The object is to remember items on a tray,
by associating one with another in practical ways, e.g. scissors cutting
string and paper; pens writing on paper; pens kept in a jar. You can find
these kinds of associations with objects located next to each other.

Repeating
Write out the information you want to learn several times. This can
help with spelling words, learning tables, learning definitions and dates
when events occurred.

Repeat aloud several times. Do this to learn tables, quotations,
poems and other extracts from literature.

Listen several times to a record or tape. Read into the tape recorder and
replay it to yourself several times. Listen to it as you fall asleep at night.

Re-read information several times. By itself this is not as effective as
when coupled with a questioning and/or association technique.

Testing yourself

Using a **basic revision method** (pages 63–64), **key word revision cards** (pages 64–68) and **reviewing over time** (pages 75–76) demonstrate the importance of testing yourself in memorising.

Wherever possible, learn topics in a logical whole unit, looking for the natural breaks between topics. Where the whole topic feels too much to revise as one unit, break it down into logical sub-topics or parts.

Don't learn all the parts separately and then test yourself. Build up your learning by revising the first part and testing yourself on it before revising the second. Test yourself on the first two parts before moving on to the third part and so on.

Finally, you are likely to recall most readily:

– the facts you learn first (*primacy*).
– the things you work at most frequently (*frequency*).
– the topics you have studied most recently (*recency*).
– topics you worked at with maximum *concentration* and *intensity*.

Forming a link to places

Create a picture in your imagination to which you link facts. This can be real or imaginary. If you use a real scene you could imagine your room, the kitchen, your street or other familiar places, associating particular facts with particular objects. You can have several different places and associate a topic with each.

You could also use a technique the Romans and Greeks used for remembering. They imagined themselves walking through a palace and pausing at particular doors, stairways or passages associating them with particular objects.

You can do the same in your own home by:

• placing a particular topic you wish to remember in a particular location

• keeping your study of particular subjects or particular topics to a particular room or chair, using your senses to the full to enable you to experience fully studying that topic in that place and time

• keeping your notes and books for particular subjects or topics in their specified area of your home; thus when you picture that place you access memory of that subject

• placing an item you wish to recall in a distinct and entirely new environment and associating it with that unique place.

CREATING A BETTER MEMORY

Nine steps to a better memory

1. Use it regularly. The more you give your memory to do, using appropriate approaches for you, the better it will function.

2. If you want to remember something then find a clear link with something about which you already know or have some knowledge or understanding. Draw upon past experiences to make links with the new information.

3. Be positive. Believe you can learn and remember it. Set out to enjoy learning and to find the most sensory useful as well as enjoyable techniques that suit you.

4. Remember pictures. Most people underuse their visual memory. For example, if you are trying to remember an address, make pictures of the street and imagine walking down it, pausing to look at the road sign and the colour of the door, with the number on it. If you do not know the place invent a picture to go with the address.

5. Use all your senses to make a picture. Hear, smell, touch, taste as well as see the object – or at least use as many of these senses as is realistic.

6. Understand your own best memory triggers. Use this chapter to identify your own best remembering techniques.

7. Build up your memory little by little, linking each 'nibble' of learning with things you have already experienced and can understand.

8. Learn facts in groups of no more than two or three. Build on this by making links to another group of two or three items. Only learn four or more items together when they make complete sense as a whole group of items.

9. Most importantly, review the new information regularly, actively recalling the last item you learned. Do so at regular intervals.

Reviewing over time

Here are four examples of the principle of regularly reviewing what you have learned as a fundamental tool of improving memory. It does not matter which you choose. Try to find one that works for you.

Example A

1. Review or revise for one hour.

2. Take a break, 10 minutes later, review for another 10 minutes the key points in any notes *or* write down what you can remember in key notes.

3. The next day review these notes for 5 minutes.

4. Review again in about a month for another 10 minutes. (You may be unsure you will remember the notes for that long – although you have a very good chance of doing so. In which case build in a check after one or two weeks.)

Example B

Revise	1	For up to one hour
Review	2	Later that day
	3	The next day for 2–3 minutes
	4	The next week
	5	The next month
	6	Six months later.

Example C

Revise	1	For up to an hour
Review	2	Immediately afterwards
	3	The next day for ten minutes
	4	Two or three days later
	5	Two weeks later
	6	Three months later
	7	Every six months afterwards.

Example D

Revise	1	For up to one hour
Review	2	After one hour
	3	The next day
	4	The next week
	5	The next month
	6	After six months.

These review periods need only be very short – 2 to 10 minutes. Whichever system you use it is the process of re-reviewing that is important.

Recalling – a four-step system

When asked to recall the events that occurred at the scene of a crime, eye witnesses often told remarkably different versions of events. An Open University programme looked at how psychologists had helped the police develop a more effective step recall process. This is the system.

1. Recall the context
Include in this where you were, what was happening, who was there, what time of day it was, what the weather was like and how you felt.

2. Seek out all that can be remembered
Include minor details however apparently irrelevant they may seem. Thus you might describe the rain on a windscreen, a piece of paper blowing in the wind, the look on the shopkeeper's face, a blue pram and so on.

3. Question specific parts of the event
Ask yourself for detailed recall of the sequence of events and the most detailed look at the colour, sound and smells in the situation including how you felt. For example, what drew your attention to the crime initially, what happened next and immediately afterwards and so on.

4. Imagine you are seeing it from a different viewpoint
That is, as if you were someone else in the situation or standing somewhere else and observing what was going on. For example, what if you had been the taxi driver, what might you have seen?

Try out this four-step system on the next topic you study as a way of reviewing your learning.

Minimising false memory
However, memory can be:

- *selective* – you miss some things out and include others
- *reconstructed* – you can put it together afterwards, perhaps in a slightly different order
- *contaminable* – you can be influenced by subsequent events and distort images, places, faces.

That is why the vivid techniques of *using all your senses* (pages 79–88) to the full, *association* (page 73) and *reviewing* (pages 75–76) are such powerful tools for your learning and minimise the chance of error occurring.

Avoid 'trying' to remember
'Try to remember' is a phrase I remember from childhood when I had lost something or had a test. It is still a phrase that I associate with someone trying to help me find something I have mislaid. I get anxious to some degree when I hear the words and that I may actually TRY to remember something. The attempt usually fails because I am too aware

of the process of trying to remember; the word 'try' does not help.

The process that works best is pleasurable and where you have no awareness of 'trying'. If you attend fully to the topic, question or task you are focused upon and then recall it – you will be checking that you have *assimilated* it, i.e. remembered it.

USING YOUR BRAIN: RIGHT AND LEFT HALVES

One of the firm impressions gained from meeting many thousands of learners is that most of us vastly underuse the capacity of our brain. Understanding the way it works – and in particular, the function of the right and left halves of the brain – can provide a stepping stone to making the best use of your brain.

The left and right halves of the brain process information in somewhat different ways. The right brain responds to art, music and patterns, processing information holistically, grasps the whole picture quickly and is more sensitive to subconscious influences. The left brain tends to work on a step-by-step basis. Most teaching is geared to the left brain.

However, the belief among many researchers into learning is that if you fully involve the right brain with the left brain – enable yourself to call on both – then you vastly increase your ability to use your brain. Making connections and associations between the functions of both halves of the brain enables you to learn and remember vast amounts of information.

Functions of the brain – both left and right

Left-side of brain
words
logic
linear sequence
analysis
number
lists

Right-side of brain
colour
spatial relationship
awareness of space, e.g. depth
distance, dimension
imagination
dream images
pattern
Gestalt (whole) see page 35

What are you better at?

If you are more on this *left-side* you are likely to be better at:

If you are more on this *right-side* you are likely to be better at:

Writing	Drawing
Recognising digits, number and combinations	Verbal materials, spoken or written; where you can use or see pictures

Recognising and recalling words	Using photographs and diagrams
Drawing on previously acquired, organised information	Drawing on many patterns, which come in no clear sequence but connect with images you feel.
Slower, step-by-step, analysing and detecting	Faster and wide-ranging matching up of ideas and images
Spotting differences in sound and language	Spotting differences in touch and 'feel'

USING ALL YOUR SENSES

This is a diagrammatic representation of some ways in which our senses connect.

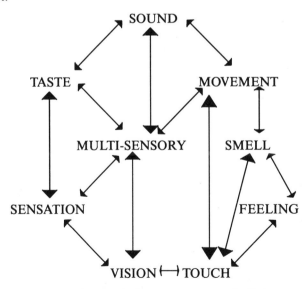

As the arrows in the diagram indicate, you can make links, connections and associations between the senses to help the fullness of your memory of the initial piece of information you set out to learn. There are a number of ideas and examples of how to make these links in the sections that follow.

Making specific links

You can make these multi-sensory associations more specific by linking them

    with numbers
    with rhythms as in Buzan's number/rhyme system (page 90)
    with letters
    with places
    with people
    with colours
    and with smells.

Choosing the words you use most often?

The words you speak can help you detect how you will most effectively learn, remember and recall a piece of information.

Over the course of a few days, notice if you use some of these words more often than others. Ask a friend or family member if they recognise your use of particular words.

visual words   *auditory/sound words*   *sensation/kinaesthetic words*

Tick off ✓ and count up the number of times you use particular words or phrases like these:

picture	hear	feel*
clear	say	touch
focus	ask	(I was) thrown
see	note	struggle (to remember)
outlook	tune (in)	hit
vision	voice	irritate
spectacle	(strike a) chord	rub (up the wrong way)
lazy	tone	run (with it)
show	(a) ring (to it)	(put your) finger (on it)
illustrate	harmony	tangible
reveal	sound	move
paint	sing	impress
		grope (for a word)

*This can be an indication of you as an emotional-connected/intuitive person as well as a 'sensation' person.

If you find yourself using words from one column a lot more than another then it can help you choose which methods to use when you are learning anything at all – either visual methods, auditory methods or active kinaesthetic methods.

You will often find it is a combination of two of these, such as visual and kinaesthetic. In which case, you could combine two approaches. Examples are:

- Draw colourful pictures and walk around the room recalling them.

- Pin your visual notes (poster-sized to A4) on a rough-surfaced wall and trace the outline of your visual notes with your hands.

- Sit in a different chair, at a different angle with a different view each time you look at particular notes.

- Sit in the same chair with the same view when you recall them. You can do the same with upright exam chairs, even in the empty exam room, to practise the recall.

If you check your *eye movement patterns* with this word list you will begin to have a clearer picture of the best learning and recall methods for yourself. You will find more about using your eyes on pages 85–87.

MATCHING TECHNIQUES TO YOUR SENSES

The lists below bring together some examples of learning techniques which draw strongly upon your visual, aural (sound) and body (physical) learning senses. There is some cross-over between them and it is certainly a good idea to combine more than one sense to enhance the intensity of the image.

Visual techniques (seeing)
- Learning maps/mind maps/patterned notes (A4, A3 or poster-sized).

- Design a poster to capture the subject.

- Use colour codes, e.g. on parts of formulae.

- Use highlight pens for new information, different categories of information, e.g. tenses in French, different types of species in biology.

- Check key word or flash cards.

- Create a flow-chart.

- Draw cartoons with facts attached.

- Add facts and information to cut-out magazine pictures.

Fig. 8. Aids to visual techniques.

- Use symbols and shapes like those in Figure 8 to give emphasis and variety.

Internal visualisations
You can also use visual techniques inside your head.

- Stop and take time to make a mental picture of what you are learning.

- Re-run a 'video' of what you have experienced through your imagination, picturing yourself in the situation and following with your video camera the sights, sounds and sensations as you move through the scene in your imagination – exactly as it happened.

- Bring up the poster you have drawn or the colourful A4 sheet of notes in your 'mind's eye' to refresh your memory.

Aural techniques (hearing)
- Make an audio-tape of a lecture, talk or TV programme.

- Explain a topic to someone else.

- Read aloud as if the topic is a drama.

- Write a jingle or a song or set what you want to remember to a suitable tune you know already.

- Talk to yourself – out loud and hear it in your head, a technique many writers use (see John Whale 1982).

- Make your own audio-tape of what you are learning, to play back to yourself in your room, on a personal stereo or in the car. It is useful for many things but excellent for languages, learning lines in plays and relaxation.

Body techniques (physical movement)
- Move around. Get up and talk to yourself as you walk.

- Write on Post-its and stick them on different objects.

- Demonstrate ideas by gesture and movement – with face, hands, arms and your whole body.

- Use quizzes and games to help you learn a topic.

- Role-play the issues with some of your peers.

- Place study materials in various places around your home.

Paying attention to detail
If you pay full attention to the detail of what you want to know or understand you will have a much better chance of recalling it.

One of the very best illustrations of how to use this insight to develop a skill is the step-by-step approach to drawing devised by Dorothy Edwards in her book *Drawing on the right side of the brain*. In it, she takes you through steps which involve you looking at an object from different perspectives such as drawing the object upside down (the object, not you) and touching the surface texture and shape of an object before drawing. She gives many illustrations of how individual people have transformed their drawing ability with such techniques (here rather briefly conveyed). I have also seen the results of people following her course from her writing: the results are impressive.

Combining sight and movement

There are two different approaches:

- You can use this combination of senses to recall what you were learning and where. An example would be creating a patterned note with coloured pens on the economic ideas of Keynes whilst dangling your feet in water (in a pool, pond, stream or the sea).

- You can also create images of things you want to remember in your imagination by trying one or two of the following:

Picturing one or more objects
speeding along
flying
dancing
stuck <u>over</u>   or alongside another
      under
folded into each other
wrapped around another word, idea, picture
one inside another
crashing or smashing into another

Finding a link with smell and taste

The technical term for smell is olfactory and the term for taste is gustatory and there is no doubt that they are powerful senses – perhaps the most powerful. We tend to overlook their importance and their potential to link with learning.

Some smells are particularly important. The perfume industry makes its fortune out of our interest and sensitivity to different fragrances. Such smells can 'turn our heads' or 'turn our stomachs' as can the smell of cooking 'make our mouth water'. You will notice that each of these phrases makes a link between smell and movement or other sensations.

Similarly some tastes are known to be particularly popular and sought after in many societies. Most people will have a reaction to bitter tastes. Imagine sucking a lemon or lime; what did you feel? Did your face move? Certainly sweet tastes spawn a huge world-wide industry of chocolate bars and sweets.

Some links between smell and sound are made accidentally such as when the smell of new-mown grass drifts to your nostrils at the same moment as you are listening to a poem in a classroom.

Devise your own list of smells and tastes to see if you can link some of them to particular pieces of information you want to remember. This could be something as simple as eating an orange or rubbing some favourite smell in the form of massage oil onto your hands as you read a passage in your book.

Moving and learning

One useful approach for connecting learning with the fullest range of your senses is to change the seat or position in which you are studying immediately after you have

- grasped some particular fact or understanding
- seen a way of applying an idea
- understood what you need to do next.

This would mean you moving around a room, occupying a slightly different position each time, ensuring that you do not return to the same place in a particular spell of study. In this way you both reinforce the learning and come to associate a particular piece of learning with a particular place.

Using several senses for peak performance

Example
After winning a gold medal in the World Athletic Championships, Liz McColgan described what she did as she ran the 25 laps of 10,000 metres. 'I switch off. I visualise myself running alongside myself and running well. I listen to my body. I concentrate on the rhythm of my breathing and body. I take no notice of the laps. Toward the end I say to myself "I wish this was bloomin' over."'

Liz listens to her own body, cutting out much of the external world.. She is also using a number of other approaches to enable peak performance. She is certainly using visualisation and rhythm, for example.

Using your eyes for visual recall

There are three parts to accurately recalling the picture that you have just seen. The three parts are:

1. Attending to it fully, checking that you know exactly how it looks by noting such things as colour; how the information was laid out; what was above and below and next to a particular piece of information. You'll find more about how to do this in **Choosing ways of remembering** (pages 73–74).

2. Remaining relaxed, calm and engaged with details of the task as you begin to recall it. Continue to notice and monitor that you are remaining relaxed and purposeful as you recall.

3. Picturing the scene by keeping your eyes upward. That is, you keep your eyes in a position above the horizon, not allowing them to drop downward. This is because visual eye movements will tend to be upward eye movements.

Most people picture a familiar scene, e.g. the inside of their bedroom, by looking to the centre or the left of the centre to recall the picture. You may find it helps to gaze into the distance, ignoring your surroundings or to close your eyes. Try it. If you try to recall the same scene with your eyes looking downward, is it as easy?

Exactly the same principle applies to spelling words accurately, for all good spellers are visual recallers. Test somebody who's a good speller and they'll either write it down on paper so they can see the word or they'll use an upward eye movement (often to the left of centre or to the centre distance) to read off the letters, or groups of letters of the word they've seen.

This is how eye movements work in aiding recall.

Recalling using your eyes
We now know that eye movements tell us how to access information. The faces in Figure 9a show you how you move your eyes to recall particular pictures, sounds and sensation.

Up or defocussed is for picturing (visualisation), e.g. picturing a page of notes; a place you know well; imagining a scene.

Down right is for feeling (sensation), e.g. you tend to look here when you are anxious or panicking; when you are recalling something you touched or tasted or smelt.

Anywhere else is for sound, e.g. talking to yourself, remembering what a tutor said, the words of a song, the script of a play.

Fig. 9a. Using eyes for recall.

Figure 9b is another diagrammatic representation of the eye movement with some more specific indications of what is happening when you move your eyes in these directions.

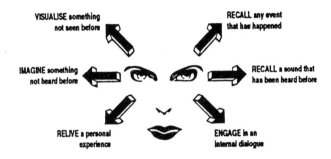

Fig. 9b. Using eyes for recall.

Using a friend to help you check eye movements
You can use a friend to help you check your own movements and can do the same for them.

- Notice that the way the faces are drawn is as if you look directly at the other person, so that eye movements which appear to be looking right on the page are actually the person looking left. Do, when you ask your friend questions, sit opposite them and notice very carefully where they move their eyes.

- Sometimes eye movements will not be clear to you, particularly if you become anxious. When you are anxious, your eyes will tend to move down.

You will remember best the information you can associate with positive images that are

- colourful
- moving/active
- 3-dimensional
- exaggerated
- funny
- distorted
- surreal
- absurd
- vivid
- sensual
- sexual
- erotic

and by associating the visual image with other senses whenever possible.

Imagining yourself as the object of your study

Example

One research scientist, Carol, has developed many of her new ideas by imagining herself as the tiny micro-organism into which she is researching. She sees herself setting out on a 'virtual-reality' journey and being faced by all the obstacles and dangers that the tiny particle will face. Partly as a result of this creativity she has become a world expert in this sphere of knowledge, contributing research papers and speaking at international conferences.

You can use this approach equally well to see yourself in the 'thick of the action' at some historical event or to imagine yourself travelling across some geographical landscape.

Shrinking the picture

One tip for the exam room is to picture what you want to recall on a tiny piece of paper.

Imagine yourself taking it into the exam room with you on the back of your hand, for example, and being able to look at it in the exam room.

It is a technique to reassure you that you can take a picture with you into the exam room, a small, vivid one, and you can do it without cheating, without actually taking in a piece of paper.

Example

Sylvia used a somewhat larger (A5) sheet of paper, but the same principle, in her OU exams:

'I would reduce my notes on a topic to an A5 sheet and in the exam I would remember what I'd written where.'

She adds – as a warning:

'But once I forgot to turn the page over, in my mind. I forgot that I hadn't room for all the information on one side of A5 and had put some extra information on the back! Annoying!'

MAKING WORD AND LETTER ASSOCIATIONS

Using mnemonic devices

The word mnemonics comes from the Greek goddess of memory Mnemosyne. Mnemonics are devised for artificially aiding the memory. There are several of these, some of which are very familiar.

Using first letter mnemonics

The colours of a rainbow/spectrum can be remembered with:

Richard Of York Gave Battle In Vain
Red Orange Yellow Green Blue Indigo Violet

Remember the sequence of:
North East South West by linking them with Never Eat Shredded
Wheat

This can be combined with a visual image, moving clockwise around
the circle.

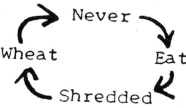

The use of the first letter in a word to construct a more vivid,
memorable sentence is used in several science subjects, e.g. Biology, as
well as in subjects like history and economics. *Words* can also be made
from first letters.

Linking mnemonics with humour
A mnemonic device with a slightly humorous or vulgar slant can be
used to link one idea with another, as in:

'Rene Descartes was a silly old fart
Who said I think therefore I am'

In this case linking a name of someone (Descartes) with an idea ('I
think therefore I am'). You can use it equally well to link names with
inventions or incidents and in physical or human science to link names
with objects.

Using raps
Some find making up a rap to go with a particular piece of learning is a
helpful, rhythmic way to learn a particular passage.

Example
Wendy tried a rhyme after watching an 'Accelerated Learning' video.
She made a tape recording of the six verses:

Get yourself mentally prepared,
It's no good, to tear out your hair,
Get a focus, relax your mind,
Motivation you must find.

Information is what you need,
Flick through the book you wish to read,
Draw yourself a concept map.
It's another feather in your cap.

Explore the subject, use your brain,
Your understanding won't be in vain,
Why not teach other things?
Who knows what this could bring.

Your memory must now kick in,
The key points will begin to this,
Imprint them on the back of your mind,
So when recalled you can find.

Now you've got to show you know,
Give your work that feel of flow,
You're judging just how well you've done,
It's not a drag; it's meant to be fun!

Look back on what you've achieved,
Yes! There's cause to be relieved,
Assess the process, what went well?
Next time you do it, it'll be real swell!

Learning rhymes
Familiar uses are for days of the month, 'Thirty days hath September, etc.', and in the spelling rule 'i before e except after c'. You can invent your own rhymes or use those which exist already in a particular subject.

Using spelling association
Where there is a confusion between the spelling of similar sounding words with different meanings, the correct spelling can be remembered by associating the spelling with that of an associated object, e.g. stationary and stationery: station<u>e</u>ry and <u>e</u>nvelopes.

When writing, I remember whether to use the word practice or practise by knowing that the two earlier letters in the alphabet go together, as do the two later ones, i.e. c and n / s and v:

practi<u>c</u>e and <u>n</u>oun, e.g. I went to the football practice
practi<u>s</u>e and <u>v</u>erb, e.g. I practise deep breathing daily.

Experimenting with number rhyme systems
This device is explained in Buzan (1989). A number is associated with an object with which it rhymes, e.g. four/door; five/hive. To remember

a piece of information you link it with the number rhyme and create a picture which is as vivid, bizarre or humorous as possible involving the piece of information with the door or hive as the case may be.

Making verbal association

- *Group words* together, e.g. to remember port and starboard and their coloured lights on a boat:
  Right – Starboard – Green are the three longer words,
  Left – Port – Red are the three shorter words.

- *Pair words* – Seek words that match/complement each other or are opposites to each other in order to aid the memory of both.

- *Link words and phrases* with those already known to you.

- *Unlikely associations* – Look for humorous, bizarre, exotic and colourful associations between facts, ideas and other information. Opposites can also be used as an aid to memory.

- *Make up a story* – Form several words you want to remember into a story. The words appear in the story in the same sequence as you wish them to appear in answer to a question.

Using tape recordings to aid memory as you go to sleep

As you go to bed at night you can use a tape recorder or personal stereo to play back some study ideas you have previously recorded. This is an opportunity to review the work you have been doing.

You can choose to add music to aid the absorption of what you have recorded by using the dubbing feature of a stereo system to record your voice over a previously recorded rhythm and/or soothing piece of music.

If you fall asleep whilst listening to some study material it may help your subconscious mind make links and associations in sleep. If sound in particular is an important way for you to access information, this technique may be worth trying: check your recall the following day and ask yourself, 'How much do I remember?'

REVISING AND REMEMBERING FOR PROBLEM-SOLVING SCIENCE AND TECHNOLOGY SUBJECTS

Repetition and mnemonics can both be used to learn formulae, tables, sequences, etc. Other memorising ideas will suit particular topics or questions. Other particularly useful approaches are:

- To practise answering questions, both in *full* and in *outline*. Do this as often as possible. Worked examples and questions are a key approach in problem-solving subjects.

- From an early stage, reduce the amount of time you allow yourself so that by the time you are close to the examinations you are allowing yourself no more time that you would have in the exam room.

- Practise diagrams and any other visual material without looking at the original book or notes. Upon completing them compare them with the original, repeating the process until you can draw an adequate representation of the original without errors.

- Use key word revision cards to practise recall of formulae, symbols, etc. and for keeping your diagram outlines.

- Let your imagination take off: picture yourself telling the story of the experiment, or how atoms interact by a fully financed major documentary. You can go anywhere and find any people, places, equipment or graphics you need to make a film that will vividly convey what scientist Dr Carol Turley calls the story-line.

- If you were making this documentary you would need a story-board, which is the sequence of the story-line, told in pictures. You would normally do these as small sketches, several to an A4 sheet, but you could also create a bigger image on poster-sized paper.

- Create a colourful poster. Group formulae together by colour codes – using colour to highlight *similarities* and *differences*.

UNDERSTANDING AND REMEMBERING MATHS

Mathematics often makes sense if you picture the problem (upward eye movements) before you start to answer it. You could also make some guess as to the answer and as you work on it as to its conclusion. See how far off the correct answer you were initially. Here are some further ideas:

- For learning formulae and other data, try creating the vivid and absurd images described on pages 88–89. You will find many concrete examples in Harry Lorayne (1992) (see **Further Reading**).

- As you read maths questions, ask yourself 'What have I got to do with this?' The question-setter wants you to be able to unpick whatever has been set. As one Chief Examiner at GCSE put it 'Unpick the knitting to turn it into common-or-garden maths.' If you carefully read the question, circling key information and using coloured highlight pens, you will have made a good start by unpicking it.

- Use mnemonics like SOCATOA (say it aloud) for
    <u>S</u>ine – <u>O</u>pposite
    <u>C</u>osine – <u>A</u>djacent
    <u>T</u>angent – <u>O</u>pposite and <u>A</u>djacent

- Get used to writing out your workings in full even when you have used the calculator, by doing so after each step of the calculation. You can do this in pencil initially, because some mistakes almost inevitably occur. When you have the correct answer, you can write it out in full, in ink. From GCSE exams onwards, up to four out of every six marks can be given for those written workings and examiners say one of the most common mistakes is to miss them out.

Example
In a TV programme, Bob, now a chief examiner for maths GCSE, spoke of one of his experiences of a maths exam when he was a student:

'I actually took a maths exam in which I got the answer wrong in every single question – but still passed because I got all the working right.'

- Maths is a 'building-block' subject in that you need to understand the bottom bricks in the wall before you can fit other ones onto them. It is best to start your revision from the points where you last clearly understood a particular 'brick' and how it fitted into the wall. Build up your confidence in a bit-by-bit 'brick-by-brick' way.

Seeing, touching and learning
You can improve your understanding of a subject if there is an opportunity to see and touch a three-dimensional model.

Example
Bill, a podiatry student studying the bones of the foot for an examination to become a chiropodist, took home a model of the foot to practise on. By touching bones and seeing how one related to another, he was able to understand complex information more easily than in a drawing or two-dimensional diagram on a page.

Learning tables
In both maths and science you may find it helpful, even essential, to learn tables of information such as your *times tables*. Here are some approaches that may help you do it more effectively.

- Get an overall picture. Write out the tables on large sheets (even poster-sized) pieces of paper. Use different colours to indicate
    - those you know already (you usually do not have to start from scratch)

– the ones you are going to learn next.
You can update this by changing the colours when you know you are able to recall it.

- Co-operate with someone else by saying the tables out loud. Sing or chant (in a rhythm) any parts you can.

- Record the tables onto a cassette and play them back to yourself, taking a section at a time.

- Cut up the tables into sections and spread them on the floor, tackling one at a time and forming a pile of those you now know.

- Walk around as you tackle or look at the information.

- Keep going over the information until you are sure you know it (repetition).

- Make up cards for parts of the tables and play test-yourself games – by yourself or with another person.

- Do not be bothered by the mistakes you make when learning them. If you make a mistake, find some simple 'soft and gentle' technique for picking it up, e.g. a smile to yourself, a little whistle.

WANTING TO KNOW MORE?

You will find more about the techniques described in this chapter in the books and videos mentioned at the end of this book, in particular those by Dorothy Edwards, Tony Buzan, Joseph O'Connor and John Seymour, and Colin Rose, which cover such fields as drawing, mind-mapping, effective use of the brain, neuro-linguistic programming and accelerated learning.

5
Taking Exams

MINIMISING EXAM DIFFICULTIES

In some ways you could argue that the first external-type examinations you take are the most difficult because they are unfamiliar and you have had little or no opportunity to develop any expertise in taking them. This would usually be GCSE exams such as French oral or Grades in music examinations. Many mature students returning to degree-level study in higher education find their first internally marked examinations cause them difficulties because they too are unfamiliar with exams after a long break from taking them.

You can minimise the unfamiliarity of these exams by simulating exam conditions and practising examination-type question and answer before you sit the exam: for many students, with experience and appropriate techniques, they can become easier. Overall, the difficulty of all examinations is exaggerated: exams are easier than is often believed.

KNOWING YOUR EXAMINATIONS

One way of checking that you know what each examination requires of you is to answer the following questions, where they apply to a subject.

1. How many papers do you have to sit?
2. What time is allowed for each paper?
3. How many questions do you have to answer? How many questions are there to choose from?
4. Do you have to answer questions from particular sections?
5. Are there any compulsory questions?
6. Are all questions worth equal marks? If not, which questions are worth more?
7. What is the maximum time you could allow yourself for each question in order to divide your time equally?
8. How are marks proportioned between coursework (C), laboratory (L) or workshop (W), project work (P) and examinations (E)?
9. Are marks linked between one year's examinations and another? (This occurs more frequently in some further and higher education exams.)
10. How long, at maximum, could you allow yourself for preparation of each question, e.g. jotting down some outline answers?

If you don't know the answers to these questions, check with teachers and past papers, ensuring no changes have occurred since the last time candidates sat the examination.

Recording exam information

You can use the blank boxes in Figure 10 to write down your answers to the above ten questions for each examinable subject. Sub-divide subjects where there is more than one paper. The two examples are given as guidelines.

MAKING CONTINGENCY PLANS

It will benefit you to make plans before the exams begin, particularly if you anticipate difficulties.

Health

Health issues are one obvious example where you can sometimes anticipate difficulties.

Knowing your examination	Number of papers to sit?	Time allowed for paper?	Number of questions to answer? Number of questions to choose from?	Questions from particular sections?	Any compulsory questions?	Some questions worth more marks?	Maximum time for each question?	% the exam(s) contribute to subject result?	Marks linked to previous exams?	Maximum planning time per question?
Question No. on p. 96	1	2	3	4	5	6	7	8	9	10
Example 1 Mathematics	1	2½hr	10/14	Sect A-4 Sect B-3 Sect C-2	No	Equal	12-15 mins	E 100%	No	2 mins
Example 2 Geography	1	3 hrs.	5/9	Sect A-1 Sect B-2 Sect C-2	Q1 Sect A	Q1 = 40% Others = 15% ea.	Q1- 50-60 mins Others = 20-25 mins	P = 20% E = 80%	Yr 1 = 30% Yr 2 = 70%	5-8 mins
Your exam subjects										

Fig. 10. Recording exam information.

CHECKLIST: YOUR EXAM PROBLEMS

I have/may have problems with:	Tick if it applies to you	Brief tips	Where to find out more (pages)
Knowing enough about what I have to do in the exams		Check you know the number of papers, questions and instructions to candidates. Are there any changes this year? Speak to your teachers/lecturers.	96 97
Getting started in the exam		Read instructions carefully. Read carefully through all the exam paper. Underline important words. Make brief answer plans.	110–111 113–114
Knowing which question to answer first		Most students answer their best question first. Examiners agree that this is a good idea.	112
Never having taken such an important exam before		You don't have to be brilliant to pass exams. Be positive. Know the standard expected of you beforehand.	102–104
Settling down in the exam room		Be methodical. Read instructions: have pens, etc. ready. Read all questions. Learn some relaxation techniques in case they are needed.	100–101
Getting used to taking exams		Practise answering old exam questions in exam conditions with the same amount of time as in the exam.	101–102
Knowing what examiners are looking for		Examiners are looking to give marks, not to take them away. They are looking for answers that actually answer the question.	106
Knowing how much time to give to each question in the exam		Take away at least 30 minutes of a 3-hour exam for reading instructions, choosing questions, planning answers, etc. Divide the rest of the time equally.	97
Fearing I will not be able to answer any questions when I read through the exam paper		This is often caused by reading through the paper too quickly. Read it again underlining all important words in each question. Learn to think more positively.	113–114
Making sure I read each question properly		Underline words in questions. Try writing brief outline notes (linear or patterned) as a first answer to the question.	111—114
Wondering if I know enough to pass		Use the symbols described in **Choosing what to revise**. Concentrate on what you are doing, not on worrying.	49–50
Wondering if I will be penalised for my spelling, handwriting or use of grammar		It is important to be legible with the minimum of grammar and spelling errors but examiners are often instructed not to penalise this unduly in exams.	112 122
Not being able to write fast enough; running out of time		Write in shorter sentences if you struggle to express yourself. Most people run out of time: timed questions will minimise the effect of doing so. Exercise your fingers – A Do-it-Yourself Guide to Muscular Relaxation.	118–119 152–157
Not answering all questions in full		If time is running out, answer two half-questions. This can gain more marks than one longer answer and a missed question.	112 119–120
Planning outline answers in the exam room		Practise this technique in revision as part of testing yourself. You do not have to write these outlines but they often help.	111 112 114

Suffering from hay fever?

If you are a hay fever sufferer you are particularly at the mercy of the pollen count in the summer examination months of May and June.

You are likely to be given medical guidance by your GP which would include some combination of tablets, nasal spray and eye drops. There may still be some problem of drowsiness associated with taking some of these products; it is worth checking this with your doctor.

Even with the best preparation you may still find yourself on a hot day with a high pollen count when the windows are open in the examination room and someone starts cutting the lawn outside. If some such event occurs or you do suffer from drowsiness because of your medication, make sure you inform the invigilator at the end of the examination and the appropriate examination board. They can take such problems into account once your paper is marked.

Suffering from period pains

Period pains would be another example where medical help beforehand, e.g. pain killers, may reduce problems.

It may be appropriate as well to inform your examination centre, i.e. normally your school or college, if your symptoms are apt to be severe. They are able to inform the examining boards of any information you pass on. Your papers will be marked in the usual way and then any information from the examination centre will be considered. Exactly the same principle applies to illness that occurs in the examination room.

Tell someone if you're not well. There may be a system in your school, college or university where you can fill in a form to inform key people.

Temporary or permanent disability

The same system which operates for sufferers from hay fever or period pains also applies to those with a disability. Your examination centre, which is most often a school, college or university, will have a series of procedures which the examination board will stipulate have to be followed for those with disabilities. Special facilities may need to be provided to prevent you from being further disadvantaged relative to your non-disabled peers. You will need to apply for or request such facilities in relation to your exams and present acceptable evidence, medical and/or educational. This may involve:

- additional time in examinations (typically 10–15 minutes per hour)

- a special room in which to be examined

- a scribe or reader for those with sensory disablement or limb mobility problems

- the use of a computer

- special access to your seat or a specific position in the examination room for wheelchair users or those suffering particular emotional/medical conditions.

Each examination board will have its own very specific regulations in relation to specific disabilities. They will govern temporary disabilities such as a broken limb as well as disabilities involving severe ill health, mobility difficulties, sensory problems (e.g.hearing loss or sight loss), epilepsy and dyslexia.

Key tips
- Ensure you gather your evidence and apply as early as possible for any help.

- Gain support from key tutorial and centre staff to help represent your situation.

- Make use of any disability advisory or support service available to you.

Equipping yourself
Get ready any spare pens and any other equipment you need the day before. Put them in the bag you will take with you to the exam next day. There are usually clear guidelines as to what equipment you can take with you into exams, so check this beforehand.

Your exam equipment checklist

Item	*Needed for which exam*
Pens – black/blue	_____
– other colours	_____
Pencils	_____
Ruler	_____
Sharpener	_____
Eraser	_____
Tippex	_____
Special equipment permitted/ needed, e.g. calculator	_____
Tissues	_____
Sweets/mints	_____
Any medication needed	_____

For maths-type examinations from GCSE onwards, you will need equipment such as a pencil, ruler, eraser, protractor and calculator. Don't borrow another unfamiliar and more complicated calculator at the last moment. You may find you are wasting valuable time in trying to use it properly. Also with calculators, take a spare battery with you in case it chooses the time of the exam to run out of energy!

Sometimes formulae are printed on the examination paper at GCSE level. Check with your school or college to see if this is the case and which ones you are given.

Arriving late
You would normally be allowed, by most examination regulations, to enter any room up to half-an-hour late, if you find yourself delayed. *If you do arrive late*, do not allow yourself to be panicked. Stick to a revised and foreshortened time budget with the aim of attempting *all* the questions you have been asked to complete.

Knowing the place and time
Finding out exactly *where the exam is held*, how long it takes to reach the place, and exactly what time the examination begins and ends will enable you to plan in advance. For example, you will be able to note actual times for reading the paper, answering the first question, beginning the second and subsequent questions.

Coping with anxiety
Learning and practising the *relaxation, positive thinking and panic coping* techniques in the **Coping with Anxiety** chapter will also prepare you for all eventualities in the examination room.

GETTING USED TO EXAMS

Although some people appear to take examinations in their stride, for the rest of us the feelings associated with examinations make it very difficult to get used to them. However, if we can familiarise ourselves with what is expected of us beforehand, it may well help to lessen their impact upon us and enable us to cope better in the examination room.

Knowing what the examination examines
Use the guidelines in **Knowing your examinations** (page 97) and **Recording exam information** (page 98) to get a clear picture of the structure of the examination.

Add to this conversations with teachers/lecturers for their guidelines; looking at the syllabus (when it is available); surveying all your notes and other work from the course; reviewing past exam papers and making use of the ideas in **Devising questions around a topic** (page 52).

Practising answering questions in examination conditions

Simulate examination conditions by answering a question *in silence without* the aid of *books or other materials; at a desk* and within strictly applied *examination time limit*. You can do this for:

- individual questions
- a whole paper (2, 2½ or 3 hours)
- planning outline answers (linear, spider or patterned notes).

This will provide practice at thinking clearly and quickly in examination conditions. You may wish to try these approaches gradually, e.g. giving yourself less time each time to answer the question; working for a longer silent period each time. You could add to this by:

- using a friend or parent as an invigilator, so you can get used to someone walking past you or standing behind you

- sitting in the room where you will sit the exam to get the feel of it.

Learning from mock exams or tests

Once you have completed your mock exams, engage in a full post-mortem of them by yourself or with the help of another. Whether they went well or badly, use the **Checklists** to analyse what happened. Check your revision, exam techniques and your anxiety levels. *Write down* the changes you will make and start to put them into operation immediately.

Knowing the standard expected of you

You don't have to be brilliant to pass examinations or to do very well in them. Here are some guidelines to help you:

Standards expected
- Comments as well as marks on your work during the course.

- Any examples of model answers by lecturers, teachers or examination boards. These may also come from good answers to questions by other students known to you.

Standards that students have used
- The average student who completes an average amount of course-work, expends an average amount of effort and develops an average understanding should pass the exam.

- By revising half the syllabus, you may well be able to answer around half the questions in the exam. If you are only required to answer half the questions on the paper and you gain half-marks on each question, you will pass.

Neither of these two guidelines is exactly accurate. They could, in fact, be misleading. If the 'average' students in your group have not yet achieved a pass standard in their work, the first guideline is unlikely to be true. It is possible to revise half the syllabus but omit to revise some of the most important, and frequently occurring, topics in which case the second guideline is unlikely to be true. There are, too, other exceptions, e.g. certain medical or taxation professional examinations where a high degree of technical knowledge and understanding is demanded.

However, the *spirit* of these two statements is very useful. It is that *the vast majority of examinations are not as difficult as students believe them to be.*

Learning from the examiners
One examiner's point confirms the importance of **asking questions**.

'A worrying number of candidates totally misread the question and thus misdirected the answer.'

'The most persistent weakness was a failure to answer the question actually asked: too many candidates preferred to answer the question they would have liked to have been asked or even just put down everything they knew.'

Other examiner's comments
'Students tend to make the same mistake every year. They look at a question and answer something which is nearly the same – but not the question we're actually asking.'

'Things you "might like to" include is a useful starting point when you are a bit panicky or lost for ideas when you start planning your answer.'

'The question itself often contains information which is there to help you. It wouldn't be there unless it was needed – and it's very obvious when it's being ignored!'

'From the examiner's point of view a "good question" is one that lets the student know exactly what to do and how to do it.'

'I see so little evidence of careful answer planning.'

'I wish I could stop candidates writing out the question at the head of their answers. Perhaps they find it calming, but it is entirely wasted effort, and it only makes one wonder whether they are stalling for time.'

Remember the good news
Examiners are not looking for weaknesses or inadequacies, they are looking to give marks – they want candidates to pass. The red pen is poised to tick, not to cross or slash through what you've written – to find what is competent, clear, correct, relevant and creditable.

Learning from the students

Achieving students
Emily and Victoria were both very successful at obtaining excellent GCSE grades. Afterwards they were asked why they did so well at GCSE:

Emily: 'The main reasons why I think I did as well as I did in my GCSE examinations are (1) a great deal of time and effort spent on coursework; (2) good relationships with all my teachers; (3) extra work after school; (4) extreme worry about the examinations that made me work non-stop; (5) determination to get as high grades as possible and get into A levels; (6) support from my family and teachers.'

Victoria: 'I worked very hard throughout the whole of Year 11 and most of Year 10 so I did not get really stressed and worried before the exams were about to start. I did as well as I did in my GCSEs because I worked hard and achieved good grades for coursework, which made me feel more confident about sitting the exams. I answered lots of past papers and did lots of timed essays so I got used to the types of questions that were likely to be asked.'

Three other students, Joanna, Stephanie and Holly, reviewed why they did well at their GCSEs:

Joanna: 'The main reasons I did well were (a) revision; (b) I practised exam questions; (c) I supplemented all work with extra notes.'

Stephanie: 'The main reasons why I did well at GCSE were my own personal hard work and the encouragement of particular teachers. These teachers made an effort to go through past papers and explain them.'

Holly: 'The three main reasons why I did as well as I did in my GCSE examinations were: (1) thorough revision was timetabled and I made sure I stuck to it; (2) my relationship with my parents – they encouraged me but never put too much pressure on me. They also helped me with anything I didn't understand; (3) there was no pressure from my friends to do badly.'

Friends could also have a positive effect on GCSE results:

Nicole: 'I found that friends encouraged me to work harder by telling me they had started revising, encouraging me to revise as well.'

Chloe: 'The main reason why I think I did as well as I did in my GCSE examinations is that I have friends with high standards like me which I feel encouraged me quite a lot.'

Under-achieving students
In a survey of 125 Year 12 and Year 13 students at one school which has GCSE results well above the national average, the students reviewed their GCSE experience. The students were asked to offer answers to the statement: 'I under-achieved at GCSE because...'

- 37 per cent of girls and 45 per cent of boys offered 'I did not do enough revision' as the main reasons for under-achievement.
- 16 per cent of the sample felt that the influence of their friends was an important factor in their under-achievement, particularly in relation to the amount of revision completed.

Just as friends can have a positive effect on results, so they can also have a negative effect, especially where boys are concerned:

Edmund: 'When it came to revision and homework or friends, going out with friends was always more appealing.'

However, some like Michael managed to resist the negative effect of peer pressure, which can be considerable:

Michael: 'The behaviour of the others rarely affected me as I got on with what I needed to do.'

DISPELLING IRRATIONAL BELIEFS ABOUT EXAMS

Here are six common beliefs that are held about exams and their outcome, all of which have some elements of false assumption or irrationality in them.

KNOWING WHAT EXAMINERS WANT – AND DON'T WANT

Examiners DO want	Examiners DO NOT want
To give marks. Examiners are often teachers and lecturers sympathetic to students. In many internal exams they will be your own lecturers and teachers, with good reason to seek to award you marks.	To take marks away. (Examiners are not poised with pens ready to penalise your mistakes.)
You to pass.	You to fail.
You to answer the question that has been set.	Waffle and bluffing which may irritate them: to be told all the candidate knows about a topic, whether it answers the question or not.
You to present the best of what you have done.	To know what you haven't done.
You to demonstrate what you understand and its relevance to the question.	You to write all you know about a topic when it does not answer the specific questions.
Scripts to be legible. They have a large number to read in a short time with the same fee for each script.	Illegibility. See **Writing Legibly**. (page 122)
All the required number of questions to be attempted.	Extra questions to be attempted. Not only do they not gain more marks, but the reverse is usually true as answers tend to be shorter. Fewer than the required number of questions to be attempted. They are disappointed for the candidate.
Short, simple sentences and a direct style of writing.	Over-elaborateness, over-wordiness.
Opinions to be backed by relevant argument.	Unsubstantiated opinion, i.e. 'I think' or 'I believe' without adequate explanation or argument for the belief. In Social Science, the use of 'I. . .' in this manner is frequently frowned upon and opinions are expressed impersonally.
All parts of a question to be answered.	You to neglect the second part of a question, which is frequently worth the same marks as the first part. (A common fault of candidates.)
Appropriate examples and illustrations.	A catalogue of examples before a point is properly explained.
Standard English.	The use of slang or spoken expressions, particularly at the beginning of sentences, e.g. 'Yes, you can please some of the people. . . ', 'Well . . .', 'As I was saying. . . '.
You to answer the question immediately you start to write.	You to copy out the question, unless you are specifically asked to do so. Long background introductions to the topic.
Humour – intentional or unintentional!	To be bored by a candidate who has evidently put in little effort.
A structure to your answer, i.e. a beginning, middle and end with a number of separate paragraphs in written answers.	A written answer without paragraphs, lacking structure or a clear story-line.

Fig. 11. What examiners want.

Other guidelines are provided in **Writing essay-type answers** (page 117).

My future will be ruined if I fail/don't get the grades I want

Examinations are an important way in which professional groups in our society select for their membership. Success in them does open doors to particular jobs and careers. Lack of success will mean certain jobs and careers are not immediately open to you, at least at the level of entry you originally intended. Some may be closed altogether.

However, happiness, wealth, peace of mind, rich experience of life, meaningful status in the eyes of others, a worthwhile career, a useful job and an inner sense of purpose and self-belief as a human being, do not depend upon examination results. The world is teeming with people who have found that to be the case whether they passed examinations or not.

I am not lucky with exams

Some people do appear luckier than others at games of chance, with acquiring money, in making relationships or in achievements. There is certainly an aspect of chance involved in which questions appear on the examination paper compared to those you have chosen to revise.

However, examination technique can be learned very effectively by anybody and the element of luck reduced to a minimum. Practising what you have to do in the exam room is the key, as Arnold Palmer, one of the most successful golfers of all time, is quoted as saying: 'The more I practise, the luckier I seem to get.'

I'm just no good at exams. Some people are; I'm not

There are two elements in this view. One is that our past performance will determine any future attempts. The other is that in comparing yourself to others you find your performance inadequate. The answer to the first element is that the past frequently *is* escapable. By buying this book and reading this page, you have set out to become 'good at exams'. Other people are largely irrelevant. They do not depend for their success upon your lack of success or vice versa.

Exams get more difficult as you work your way up

Difficulty is a relative word. What is difficult at one age is not at another; what is difficult when you are inexperienced in an activity is not when you are experienced; what is difficult to one person is not to another; what is difficult on one day is not on another.

Certainly, examinations demand more specialist knowledge, understanding and expertise, as you move through their different levels. They may become more technical, involve more abstract ideas and concepts, involve you in greater specialisation and more specialist jargon. This does not mean they become more difficult.

I haven't covered the syllabus so I won't pass

It isn't irrational to fear that you haven't revised or understood enough of the subject you have studied to pass a course. It may be true that if you have studied and revised little of the course you have left yourself at risk of failing to accumulate sufficient marks to pass it. It may be that you will need some luck in the choice of questions that appear in the exam paper.

However, it is irrational to believe that if you haven't covered the syllabus you are inevitably going to fail the course. Few courses, teachers or students 'cover the syllabus' in the sense of paying full and equal attention to all parts of it. Examiners do not expect you to have done so. They accept that there are bound to be areas where you are underprepared, unclear or uninformed. They want to see you demonstrate what you do understand and what you have prepared.

Even when you are struggling to find enough questions to answer, you will find that many have some kind of link or association with your course content. You will normally find some links which you can build up into an answer.

The exams will expose me as a phoney or stupid

You may experience the common fear in many students that the exams will expose them as inadequate, lacking in even basic know-how or understanding. There is a further underlying fear – that the exams will expose your lack of ability to be tackling that level of study, whether it be GCSE or post-graduate qualifications. The fear can be further intensified by fantasies of the judgement by examiners, tutors, family and friends. Examiners can be seen as poised with red pens to expose your ignorance and misunderstanding. You may feel that family and friends see you as stupid or that tutors will reject you as they feel let down or fooled.

As I have argued in Chapter 1, the focus on ability is largely irrelevant. The vast majority of people who set off on a course of study are quite *capable* of successfully completing it. It is practical life circumstances, false beliefs and negative attitudes which, coupled with poor study techniques, may cause the problems – not lack of ability.

USING THE LAST FEW HOURS

Preparing the night before

- Review your key word cards with the emphasis on practising recall. Attempting to cram in *new* material, although tempting, will tend to use up energy and be self-defeating.

- Check you have all the equipment – pens, pencils, instruments, etc. you need and are allowed to take into the exam room. Several different shaped pens may ease the pressure points on your fingers and thumbs.

- Check the timetable as to the right time and place of the exam. Make sure you have any candidate's number or any other administrative items you need.

- Check your personal timetable for the next morning, checking the times you need to get up, gather your materials, leave the house, etc.

- Use any of the ideas you have developed from the **Coping with Anxiety** chapter to aid your relaxation and to sleep.

Organising yourself on the day of the examination
- Try as far as possible to stick to your normal routine.

- If you do normally eat breakfast, take it as normal for you will be using up a considerable amount of energy. If you don't eat breakfast normally, consider eating something light. If this does not seem possible, you could consider taking some glucose tablets, barley sugar or mints with you for the examination room: for most external examinations unobtrusive sweet sucking would be permitted.

- Don't drink too much in the morning. Part of the normal reaction to exams is a state of appropriate nervous tension and arousal you may feel. This may well cause more visits to the lavatory than usual, which is a perfectly normal – and appropriate – reaction. You don't, however, want the need to continue in the exam room, if it can be avoided!

- Check your personal timetable made the night before to ensure all is going to time, occupying spare time you have constructively by doing something positive or relaxing.

- Check you have all your equipment before you leave home. See **Your exam equipment checklist** (page 100).

- You can take brief looks at your revision card summaries, re-checking your recall.

- Use the deep breathing and other relaxation techniques when you feel the need for them. You may also find the ideas in **Making your way to the Exam** and **Preparing on the morning before an afternoon exam** helpful (pages 141–142).

STARTING YOUR EXAM

Getting settled

Settle and compose yourself. Set out any pens, pencils, rulers, erasers, and other permitted equipment. Check your watch with the clock in the room, which should be visible to you. If it is not visible to you, place your watch where you can easily see it. This is the moment to practise all the ideas for positive alert performance described in the **Coping with Anxiety** chapter, e.g. **Visualising taking the exam** (page 160).

Treating yourself well

You can also work out little treats as a strategy in the exam room. Sylvia did so in her OU exams.

Sylvia's treat

'My treat and confidence-giver every OU exam was a bar of Kendal mint cake. I thought if it gave mountain climbers energy, it would help me, so between questions or when I felt in need of a break I'd have a square or two (ready broken and neatly laid at the top of my desk before the exam started so I didn't distract anyone with the noise of breaking it!).'

Reading through the exam paper

Read right through the exam paper. *Allow yourself at least five minutes for this. In particular, re-check that the instructions are as you expected as in* **Knowing your examinations** (page 97), **Recording exam information** (page 97). *Note* the length of the exam and write down the finishing time, any compulsory questions, the number of questions to be answered in total and from which sections of the paper they are to be selected.

If you tend to be anxious about finding your hoped-for question appearing in the examination paper, read through the paper *not expecting* the questions you want to appear. *Expect* it to be difficult to find enough questions to answer. Adopting this approach you will probably find your hopes raised rather than dashed and it will help you look at each question much more carefully. This is not designed to be the opposite of a positive approach, simply a steadying, realistic approach.

Pay particular attention to what the question is asking. It is very easy to jump to incorrect conclusions about the meaning of a question. A common explanation for this is that anxiety to find certain topics or questions causes *a word or phrase* to be selected from a question and assumed to be the topic or particular question. We want to find certain questions so we *do* find them, whether or not they are really worded as we wish them to be! In the same way, other questions, which may well be more appropriate questions to choose, are dismissed because a key word or phrase does not appear when it is read quickly for the first time.

One way to prevent this happening is to develop the technique of **Underlining key words in questions** (pages 113–114).

One outcome of underlining can be to discover that simply worded questions are not always the easiest to attempt. Questions which require careful reading can be easier for you to answer once you have clearly understood them.

Planning your time
You can plan the outline of the time you will allocate in an exam, before the day of the examination. If you **know your examinations** and know the start and finishing times you can make a rough plan of your time allocation. During the examination itself, write down the planned finishing time for each question. Divide the time according to marks allocated per question and marks allocated per part of a question. (Increasingly, Examination Boards are including this information.)

- Stick to your time budget. As explained in **Running out of time** (page 121), two half-answered questions will usually obtain more marks than one completed question and one unanswered question.

- Use any time remaining at the end of the exam to check your answers for 10 minutes. Many students never have this checking time at the end and it is by no means essential that you plan it in.

Planning your answers
You can use brief notes to outline an answer to the question. You may decide that you would prefer to get straight on with your answer. As long as you have a clear idea of what you wish to write in your answers there is no problem with this approach. You should do what suits you best.

- You can find examples of outline notes in **Using underlined words to form an outline answer** (page 114) and in **Spider diagrams** (page 54) and **Using Pattern notes** (page 55).

- If you are using this type of outlining plan, it can be a useful approach to outline all your answers in one working spell at the beginning of the exam. Alternatively, you can plan one answer at a time or two or three together before commencing to write out your full answers. The advantage of planning all your answers at the beginning is that it enables you to record a considerable amount of information whilst it is fresh in your mind; it removes the anxiety

TECHNIQUES IN THE EXAM ROOM

The outline is expanded and adapted from one used by Rowntree in his book *Learn How to Study* (see **Further Reading**).

Settle and compose yourself
Lay out your equipment, at least two pens, ruler, pencil and other permitted equipment.

Read right through the paper (5 minutes)
Check instructions very carefully. How many questions – from each section?
Underline key words in questions.
Choose your best questions, using a symbol system.
Analyse the question very carefully, checking whether it is a 'What' or 'How' type question or a 'Why' type.

Plan your time
Divide according to marks per question.
Write down finishing time for each question.
If possible, plan in 10 minutes checking time at end.

Plan your answers
Brief notes on main ideas and important details.
Linear, spider or pattern note outline.
Outline all answers at beginning (if doubtful of remembering); or one at a time or a few answers together.
Leave space after each question.
Ignore other candidates' writing speed and spare paper collecting – it is irrelevant to your performance.

Prioritise
Answer your best question first.
Stick to the time allowed for each question: marks for two half-questions are worth more than one.
Stick to what the questions are asking.

Write
Simply, in short sentences, checking spellings.
Legibly.
Avoiding long 'background' introductions.

At the end of the exam
If there is time left, check your answers.
Minimise your post-mortems.

Fig. 12. Techniques in the exam room.

that you will forget it by the time you come to answer a later question. It also gives you notes to fall back on if you run out of time. In an emergency, you could refer the examiner to them, if they are readable and comprehensible. You can also add to these notes during the course of the exam when you think of other points you have remembered: answering one question often throws up associations with another topic or question.

- Leaving spaces after each answer will enable you to add to it, if you recall more information.

- Do not allow yourself to get stuck on a stubborn problem. Return to it later. A change of question can often enable you to gain a fresh perspective on the previous question.

Underlining key words in questions

Answering an exam question correctly depends upon understanding it clearly in the first place. A useful technique is to underline, after careful consideration, the most important words, phrases or data in the question. See below for an example.

Although you often end up underlining most of the words in a question, it is where the lines are drawn and where the spaces between lines occur which draws your attention to the exact meaning of the question.

If the words which tell you the type of question are underlined twice (or in a different colour), it will ensure you take the right approach with your answer.

In conclusion, this technique has several advantages:

- It ensures you read the question properly and note exactly what it is asking. It is very easy, in your anxiety to find a question you can answer and to get started, to misread a question. This can cause you to ignore a question which it would be quite possible for you to answer and to choose to answer a question which turns out to be different from your original perception of it.

- It draws your attention to the approach that examiners want you to take, i.e. the type of question it is.
- It provides you with the key words to start a brief outline answer plan.

Example
Q.1 <u>Give an account</u> of the <u>digestion</u>, <u>absorption</u> and <u>use</u> of <u>carbohydrates</u>.

- In order to test whether you have underlined the correct words to enable you to fully and exactly understand the question say the words you have underlined quietly aloud to yourself.
- Practise this underlining technique with questions from past papers or questions you are currently answering.

Using underlined words to form an outline answer

You can use the underlined words to form an outline answer, either in linear or pattern/spider form.

Using a patterned or spider outline

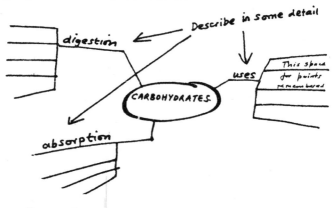

Using a linear plan

You would list the key points under headings of *digestion*, *absorption* and *uses*.

UNDERSTANDING THE TYPES OF QUESTION

Questions in examinations vary in the approach they ask you to take. In every question there are certain key words (a number of these are verbs) which tell you the type of question it is and exactly which approach the examiner wishes you to take.

Below is an A–Z glossary of such terms, some of which ask you to be more analytical, some more descriptive, in your answers.

Key words in question titles

Account for – examine

Analyse – describe, examine and criticise in great detail

Argue the case for – back your opinion by reasoning in favour of it

Assess – weigh up or judge the value of, or to what extent conditions are fulfilled

Calculate – reckon or compute by mathematics

Clarify – simplify and make clear

Comment upon – offer an opinion – give a point of view (avoid use of 'I')

Compare – look for similarities and differences between two or more objects, ideas or processes

Consider – express your thoughts and observations about

Contrast – point out the differences between

Criticise – give your judgement about merits of theories and opinions – point out defects, pass judgement, show errors – back with evidence

Define – explain in your own words

Demonstrate – show how, prove with examples

Describe – give a detailed and graphic account

Develop – expand on

Differentiate ⎱ – explain the differences between
Distinguish ⎰

Discuss – argue the case for and against

Elaborate – add details

Enumerate – make an ordered list, give main features or general principles – omit details

Evaluate – make an appraisal or find the value of

Examine – enquire into, attempt to discover, investigate, look closely into

Expand – go into more detail

Explain – make clear or intelligible, illustrate the meaning of

Explore – approach in questioning manner – consider from a variety of viewpoints

Give an account of – describe in some detail

How – in what way, by what means or method, to what extent

How far – present and evaluate evidence for and against

Identify – pick out key features (of something)

Illustrate – show, point out, make clear by use of concrete examples

Interpret – using your own experience explain the meaning of, make clear and explicit (usually using your own judgement also)

Justify – show adequate grounds for decisions and conclusions

List (name) – make a list of

Outline – give brief general description or summary without detail

Prove – demonstrate truth or falsity by presenting evidence

Relate – tell story, describe – to show how things are connected and to what extent they are alike and affect each other

Review – to make a survey of, examining the subject critically

Show – reveal, disclose (in logical sequence)

Show how – make clear by what means

State – present in brief, clear form

Summarise – make brief statement of main points

To what extent – give reasons to support argument or action

Trace – follow development or history of a topic from some point of origin. Explain stage by stage

Translate – express in different form or language

What – of which kind/which

When – at what time, on which day, year, etc.

Where – at/to what place

Why – for what reason

Verify – show to be true, confirm

Answering other types of question

Some questions combine both types of question as the examiner looks for a combination of facts and analysis, as in 'Describe and explain'.

Quotations usually indicate some kind of analysis is required.

'*Brief*' or '*List*' mean what they say. A paragraph for the first and a straightforward descriptive list, such as that above.

'*Compare and contrast*' type questions require you to point out the similarities and differences between two items, events or ideas. A good answer would focus on one aspect at a time and find the differences and similarities.

An example – Q. Compare and contrast cars and motorbikes.

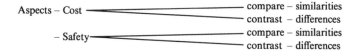

The same applies for 'For and Against' type questions, where, although you can argue all the points 'for' and then all the points 'against' separately, the answers which effectively argue for and against aspect-by-aspect can be the most successful.

In social science subjects such as history, sociology and economics, it is important to distinguish whether the examiner is asking you about the causes or reasons for or whether you are being asked about the results of events or actions.

- 'Factors', 'Account for', 'What problems faced?' – suggest you should write about reasons and causes.

- 'Achievements', 'Effects', 'Impact', 'How successful', 'The importance of' – suggest you should write about the results or consequences of an event, an idea or action.

Choosing the questions you will answer

Use some simple symbol systems to indicate your reaction to each question, once you have carefully read it and decided exactly what it is asking.

Guidelines that can be used are:

- Use a simple star system (up to 3 or 5 stars ***) next to each question: choose the questions with the highest star rating.

- Use the EASY/DIFFICULT and KNOW/UNDERSTAND symbols from **Choosing what to revise – and in what order** (page 49), choosing those questions on the positive end of the scale.

- Give the questions scores out of 10 to indicate your confidence in answering them.

- Number the questions in the order you will answer them, choosing your best question first; then second best, third best and so on.

Writing essay-type answers

You cannot exactly reproduce in the exam room an essay you wrote on the same question as part of your coursework. The time constraints in an exam are different and a more direct precise style is more appropriate for most examinations.

Here are some of the principal guidelines:

- Try to lay out your answer so that it looks attractive, particularly where your comprehension of the English language is being tested.

- Do not waste time copying out the question (unless asked).

- Write in continuous prose, not notes.

- Decide whether it is a descriptive or analytical essay you are being asked to write. Use **Underlining key words in questions** (page 113) and **Understanding the types of questions** (page 114) to help you decide.

- Keep your essay plan close by so that you can refer to it with ease.

- Avoid repetition, vagueness, generalisations and waffle.

- Use short paragraphs as well as simple, shorter sentences.

Exam essays have a beginning, a middle and an end. The beginning *Introduction* will have several of these features:

- A summary of what you are about to argue or describe.

- An indication of your attitude to the question asked.

- The key words from the question incorporated into the above, to indicate that you have read and understood the question.

- A back-up reason for any first statements made; this can be expanded upon or added to in the middle.

- Definitions of any terms that clearly need to be defined in order for you to proceed with your answer.

- It will be one or two paragraphs long.

- It will indicate that more needs to be described, explained or argued to clarify what has been said so far.

- State how you interpret the title, i.e. what do you understand by it?

- Briefly outline the ideas, factors or arguments you are going to consider and why.

But don't
- Give your answers to the questions in the title in the introduction. These fit in the conclusion.

- Simply write out the question again in your introduction but refer to the key phrase.

- Give simple dictionary definitions of terms. Use more authoritative definitions.

Writing a model essay
Introductions to essays are often of a very poor standard. Some candidates obviously get stuck in trying to express themselves. You can feel they are wondering what to write. Others simply re-state the title and say something like 'I will now go on to answer the question': a poor start. Yet others start a long, long background account of a situation, event, period, etc. before beginning to make any relevant points in answer to the question. If you find introductions to essays difficult you try some of these alternatives:

- Practise them before the exam, using the principles outlined.

- Write a very short, one or two sentence, introduction before moving on to the essential core of the essay – the middle part.

- Don't waste time thinking of 'special' things to say in an introduction. Get on with answering the question in a straightforward manner, using your plan.

The middle
The middle will normally contain your key facts. They will be expressed precisely and specifically and in as much detail as the question appears to demand. Try to avoid generalisations or covering up phrases which attempt to conceal that you can't remember a piece of information.

Assemble your major facts in a clear manner and show how they are relevant to the answer. Where the essay involves you arguing a case, citing reasons, explaining causes, analysing consequences and other forms of analysis, let the facts support your arguments.

The end – your conclusion
Concluding paragraphs are often as inadequate as introductions! As with introductions it is best not to think of them as being special concluding paragraphs.

Ideally, you will reach a coherent logical conclusion at the end of your essay. It does not have to side with any particular issue that the question focuses on. You can argue that the evidence is conflicting, the fors and againsts evenly balanced or that evidence is insufficient. Practise this type of conclusion in your preparation for the examination.

In your conclusion
- read the title again before you write it to ensure your conclusion has the emphasis the title required

- summarise the main points

- answer the question in the title or comment upon what the title required.

If you find concluding paragraphs difficult, don't over-concern yourself with them. Simply answer the question to the best of your ability and when you have done so – stop.

Finally, in conclusion, try not to start your final paragraphs with 'Finally. . .' or 'In conclusion . . .' It is boring, repetitive and tends to cause examiners to yawn!

It is important to remember that the bulk of marks in the vast majority of essay-type questions are awarded to the quality of the information and argument that forms the middle of most answers.

Answering multiple-choice questions and objective tests
The use of multiple-choice examinations is now common in pre-degree courses, although essay-type examinations remain the most common in university courses.

Multiple-choice questions, as their name implies, give you a choice of answers to a specific question. By marking a box, in the way you are instructed, you indicate which answer best fits the question. In this way, the multiple-choice exam aims to reward a good grasp of the whole syllabus without placing an undue emphasis upon the candidate's ability to write descriptive answers.

The main points to bear in mind in answering this type of question are:

- Read the instructions particularly carefully, the time you are allowed and how to complete the answers. As many of these tests and exams are marked by computer it is important that you actually complete your answers in exactly the form required.

- Work straight through the paper, noting the more difficult questions which you can return to later. Once you are sure you have the right answer, don't spend time re-considering.

- Underline key words in the questions to ensure you have read them properly. Particularly be on the lookout for *not* and double negatives in objective tests.

- Pick the alternative that appears to be nearest the truth. Multiple-choice tests are not purely tests of factual recall. They also test your comprehension and interpretation of information. One statement is going to be closest to the truth. By eliminating the answers you know to be wrong you will limit your choice and improve your chance of answering correctly.

- Don't guess randomly, but make informed guesses when you do not know. However, you should check the marking system, whenever possible, to see if incorrect answers are penalised. If penalties apply, as they do in a number of objective tests, but less often in multiple-choice papers, then be wary of guessing. Leave the difficult questions until later and return to them after completing the section. Reflecting on the question may give you some insight into the answer.

- Multiple-choice papers are not speed tests as such, but do require you to work at a business-like speed. Don't spend a long time puzzling over one or two questions. Continue on through the paper as questions you find easier may well occur throughout the paper. With other objective tests, timed sections do require that you work quickly. Keep your watch in view to time yourself carefully.

Preparing for an oral exam

The secret of good preparation for an oral examination in a foreign language such as French or in some fields of medicine is to be very thoroughly prepared.

You can do this by:

- practising the key phrases you will use to begin sentences

- practising the key information, terms and phrases you will use

- testing yourself with another person asking you questions in the role of 'the examiner'

- rehearsing as many times as you can and simulating the examination situation

- learning upward eye movements to minimise panic (see page 86)

- using your senses to the full when learning the materials (see page 79)

- starting off each of your rehearsals and preparation sessions by being in a composed state.

OVERCOMING COMMON EXAM PROBLEMS

Running out of time

Divide whatever time that remains between questions. Examiners share a wide measure of agreement that it is easier to gain five marks in the last questions than an extra five in the question you were last working on. For this reason, two half-answered questions usually gain more marks than one more completely answered question with which you have persevered.

With 10 minutes left and one answer to complete, you may revert to an emergency technique. Use brief notes to answer a descriptive (word-based) question. Minimise the amount of calculation shown in mathematically-based problem-solving subjects. (NB: This latter guideline may not apply equally to students in higher education, where showing all understanding of the means of calculation may be an important source of marks.)

Provided these brief outlines are readable and comprehensible to the examiner, they can gain marks. In most examinations, examining boards lay down criteria for marking brief notes, on a reduced scale of marks.

Alternatively, if you have written readable notes or skeleton outlines at the beginning of the examination, you can refer the examiner to them as your time elapses. If you do this, cross out the work you do not wish the examiner to read (a good principle at the end of an examination).

Writing legibly

It is a help to examiners if your handwriting is clear and readable. They will not deliberately penalise illegible handwriting, but examiners are human beings and they are going to be irritated if, because of difficulty in reading your handwriting, it takes them two or three times as long to read your script as it does to read another candidate's script of similar length, content and quality.

As with spelling and grammar, most examining bodies give guidelines to examiners as to how they should treat such scripts and, where penalties are imposed, they will tend to be only a small proportion of the total marks awarded in many examinations, e.g. 5–10 per cent.

However, even if your handwriting is not particularly legible, you could considerably improve its legibility by:

– spacing it out more
– making sure you have no two letters that look exactly alike
– avoiding loops which overlap above and below the line.

Writing style

Writing style is not a key factor in most examinations, unless it is a subject where you are examining literature or grammatical style, *eg* English Literature and Language.

You may wish to impress the examiner with the fluency of your writing and will probably do so, if you succeed. However, it is not desirable to sacrifice facts and arguments for style. Whenever you find yourself with difficulties in expressing yourself, write in short, direct, simple sentences. This is a useful guideline for most examination answers.

COPING WITH THE AFTERMATH

The problem with analysing what you write with friends or others is that, in my experience, nearly everybody is equally convinced they have missed out key facts, answered questions in the wrong way, miscalculated etc. As a result such postmortem discussions invariably reduce confidence and serve little purpose. In addition, your memory of what you wrote and its standard is likely to be imperfect, even if your recall is good. The difference between what you remember you wrote and exactly what you wrote can make a significant difference to the marks you obtain.

In some circumstances it can be useful to discuss certain issues. For example, where a subject is examined by two separate papers, the topics and types of question which appear in the first can give you guidelines to the topics and questions which may appear in the second paper.

Hoping for better results?
If you don't pass the examination on this occasion, it does not mean you're stupid or that you've wasted people's time even if some people believe that to be true. They are entitled to their misperceptions.

If you don't pass the examination with the performance you were hoping for or even expecting then over time there is an opportunity to learn from the experience by:

- looking at your learning techniques
- thinking again about your choice of course or subject
- checking over how well you prepared yourself
- examining your exam technique
and
- reviewing how you manage yourself and your lifestyle.

There is nearly always something positive you can gain from the experience. In one sense there is no such thing as success or failure, only *feedback* (information for you to act upon in the future). There are millions of people who have transformed their lives after 'failure' or disappointment; the comments in **Dispelling irrational beliefs about exams** are very relevant (pages 105–108).

6
Coping with Anxiety

UNDERSTANDING WORRY, ANXIETY AND STRESS

It is a natural human reaction to worry at times during your studies. It is also natural to express an emotional reaction to the ups and downs of tackling tasks: angry or frustrated at one time, exhilarated at another.

The ideas in this book are intended to help you avoid becoming locked into a state of anxiety, where your interaction with exams, tests and course deadlines (the potential 'stressors') results in an unhelpful stress reaction in you. This is the type of anxiety state which feels disabling.

If you have found yourself feeling overwhelmed by this form of anxiety, then there are hundreds of ideas here to help you unpick it and move you into an emotional state in which you are able to think, feel and tackle study tasks with a feeling of your own power and well-being.

Achieving optimum arousal

The trick is to find the right level of arousal. Too little or too much arousal can bring problems. What you need is to be actively involved in your own learning to ensure you are engaged enough with what you are doing to move things from your short-term to long-term memory. In doing this you can actually enjoy what you are doing; it does not have to hurt for real learning to be taking place. It can enable you to be more alert, attentive and to concentrate more fully. It can sharpen your exam performance; make you feel more full of energy; cause you to work at the most effective speed and be more attentive to detail.

It is possible to mistake this state of arousal for anxiety. It is also possible for anxiety to become disabling, i.e. to stop you working effectively or at all. Equipped with the practice of these ideas, you will be able to cope with your anxiety, no matter how severe or overwhelming it feels using brain arousal to bring you to peak performance.

The approaches are aimed at how you think, feel and behave. As well as suggestions for how to tackle any problems you may have, the approaches are grouped under main headings:

CHECKLIST: YOUR ANXIETY PROBLEMS

I have/may have problems with	Tick if it applies to you	Brief tips	Where to find out more (pages)
How anxious to be before an exam		Some tension and nervous energy can be useful to trigger you to action.	124 125–126
How to cope with panic before or during the exam		Look at *Coping with panic in an emergency*. Create a scene in your imagination and *Breathing slowly and deeply*	149 150
Being unable to concentrate		See *Improving your concentration*. Practise focusing your attention during revision, cutting out distracting sounds	26–27 164
Getting to sleep at night		Exercise, warm baths, relaxation exercises and a good sleeping posture can all be useful.	142–148
How to relax in the exam room		Learn techniques of muscle tensing and relaxing as well as how to breathe to relax	149–152 153–157 157
Whether to take some time off for relaxing and entertainment		Definitely. Incorporating time off into your revision programme is a part of your revision time not a subtraction from it.	145
Not being bothered about the exams: anxious because there is no feeling of anxiety at all		As long as you feel you are working effectively, there is no problem. If you are not, learning some effective revision and anxiety-coping techniques may free you to feel anxiety – and cope with it.	45–46 126
How to stop worrying about the amount of work to be done, what others will say		See *Coping with anxiety* and *Checking how you think* for a large number of ideas to help you.	126 130–133

- Reducing stressful thinking.
- Coping with stressful situations.
- Coping with key times.
- Getting to sleep at night.
- Breathing effectively.
- Relaxing your muscles.
- Visualising.
- Finding other approaches.

Coping with anxiety: key ideas
One or more of the following suggestions may both help you reduce anxiety and work effectively:

- Adopt positive attitudes, making positive statements to yourself.

- Stop thoughts that worry you.

- Know and adapt to situations that cause you both the most and the least anxiety.

- Rehearse and simulate situations you find difficult.

- Involve yourself in those activities which reduce anxiety.

- Learn and practise techniques for coping with panic.

- Learn skills of revising and taking examinations, e.g. how to set yourself manageable tasks and accomplish them within time limits.

- Learn relaxation techniques.

- Develop a balanced lifestyle.

- Ensure your need for sleep, appropriate diet, company, exercise and variety are met.

- Focus on tasks rather than yourself.

- Have a system for approaching problems and tasks.

- Write things down on paper rather than keeping them in your head.

- Form written hierarchies of difficulty, e.g. levels of anxiety; topics to be revised.

- Use others as helpers.

- Find out more about other helpful approaches, e.g. yoga, hypnosis.

If you have had difficulties with examinations in the past, it may help to identify the difficulties explicitly by the next exercise.

Describing your past experience of examinations

It may help you pinpoint your past difficulties to answer these questions, either in the space provided or on a separate piece of paper:

What has been your past experience of tests or exams? What kind of difficulties have you encountered?

Write down as many statements about yourself as possible which relate to any anxieties you have about taking examinations. It may help you to be specific by describing:

what you *thought*, e.g. 'I've not done enough work.'

what you *felt*, e.g. very nervous; panic.

how you *behaved*, e.g. I got stomach aches, couldn't settle down to revision; lost sleep.

Talking over the problem

Having completed answering these questions, you may wish to talk over some issues with a helper. For suggestions see Chapter 7, **Using Others as Helpers**. You can also use the **Contents** and **Problem checklists** (pages 5, 21, 45, 72, 96, 125) to seek answers to the problems you wish to overcome. You may, however, be feeling unclear about what problem to tackle or how to set about it, in which case the next exercise may help you clarify what you will do.

Tackling the problem

If you are feeling unclear about how to tackle a problem, the following four-point action sequence may help you to get started.

1. State the *problem* you wish to resolve:
   I want to. . . (This should be specific and contain an action verb, e.g. write, list, run, etc.)

2. Set a *goal*:
   So that . . . (This should be a well-formed goal statement, clear and obtainable, stating what you wish to be like.)

3. Determine an *approach*:
   So I'm going to . . .

4. Have a *plan of action:*
   How I'm going to do it . . .

Example

1. *I want to* learn emergency relaxation techniques.
2. *So that* I'm never going to 'freeze' or panic in an exam again.
3. *So I'm going to* learn 3 separate techniques, i.e. **coping with panic in an emergency, breathing slowly and deeply**, and **visualising taking the exam.**
4. *How I'm going to do it* is to read the exercises, practise them by myself and then ask a friend to help me rehearse and practise them.

You can use a sheet of paper and the same sentence beginnings, 'I want to . . .', etc., to construct your own action sequence, following the format above.

Drawing up a hierarchy of your anxiety

It may help you to understand more clearly the causes of your anxiety if you complete this exercise. Having done so, it will give you guidelines for which part of your anxiety to tackle first and subsequently.

Try to be specific and detailed, sub-dividing the situations if they have a different scale of anxiety, e.g. 'Entering the examination room' may sub-divide into – meeting friends waiting outside; finding my seat; waiting for the invigilator to give instructions; turning over the question paper.

You may wish to use the space below or a separate sheet of paper.

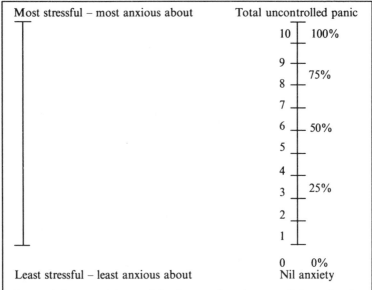

Most stressful – most anxious about	Total uncontrolled panic
	10 — 100%
	9
	8 — 75%
	7
	6 — 50%
	5
	4
	3 — 25%
	2
	1
Least stressful – least anxious about	0 — 0% Nil anxiety

It may help you understand the degree of anxiety you feel to give the different situations a score, either as a percentage or on a scale of 0-10.

Using the completed list

You have several choices. You will probably find it easiest to start with situations at the 'least stressful' end of your list, particularly if they have a low anxiety score. You can then adopt one of two approaches:

- Familiarise yourself thoroughly with that situation, simulating, i.e. recreating as closely as possible, the situation that actually causes you stress, e.g. sitting at a desk in exam conditions; walking to the exam room; writing timed answers.

- Use one of the relaxation techniques, e.g. **Guiding yourself to muscular relaxation** (page 153). Once you are in a state of complete relaxation, visualise the least stressful situation as vividly as possible. If you feel any anxiety or any tensing of muscles, then stop and return yourself to a complete state of relaxation again. If this happens at the beginning it means you have not sufficiently sub-divided your least stressful situation – you need a less stressful situation as a starting point.

Generally, you will not feel any tension as you visualise the first, least stressful situation. Having completed it, move on to visualising the second least stressful situation, and so on through your list. If at any point you feel tension you must:

- Stop and return yourself to a state of total relaxation.

- Check to see if your list needs further sub-division; if there is a smaller anxiety step you can take. You will find you can take 2 or 3 steps at a time if this is going well. Don't rush it. Enjoy the state of relaxation and the gradual reduction of anxiety.

- You may find it helpful to use a friend as a helper with this exercise.

- You will no longer feel anxious about those situations you have visualised whilst in a state of complete relaxation.

Learn and practise the exercises designed to cope with your most extreme anxiety, e.g. **Coping with panic in an emergency** (page 149), **Breathing slowly and deeply** (page 150).

Use the **Contents, Checklists**, your own questions, **Asking questions: the most important skill** (page 12), and **Tackling the problem** (page 127) to help you proceed with other anxiety items on your list.

REDUCING STRESSFUL THINKING

Checking your stressful thinking

What you find yourself thinking can both harm and help your preparation for passing exams. You may have had a bad experience which has frightened you and/or dented your confidence. This in turn can lead to you saying things to yourself which makes it difficult to prepare for exams and to concentrate on what you are studying now. You may feel frightened of the unknown and be creating a picture of something 'impossible'.

Gathered together in the checklist below (Figure 13) in the left-hand column, are many of the commonest things which, if dwelt upon in your thoughts, can create anxiety which obstructs you preparing for exams. The checklist and guidance notes which follows are designed to help you overcome these unhelpful patterns of thinking.

Using this checklist

1. Read through the whole checklist, noting points on the left-hand side that apply to you.

2. Ensure you understand the checklist by checking any of the guidance notes that follow.

3. Select 1, 2 or 3 points on the left-hand side that you now want to change.

4. Begin the process of shifting the emphasis of your thinking to the matching section on the right-hand side, e.g. from NEGATIVE self-statements to POSITIVE self-statements.

5. Practise doing, saying and focusing upon the 1, 2 or 3 things you have chosen in the right-hand column.

6. Make a note of other points on the checklist which are relevant to you. You can return to these when you are ready and follow steps 1 to 5 with them too.

7. Add this approach to others you are using to prepare for exams and manage your anxiety.

Guidance notes for reducing stressful thinking: the checklist

These notes explain why certain patterns of thinking are less likely to cause you to feel stressed.

- You cannot do anything about the past. Worrying about a problem, difficulty or failure in the past gives it too great an emphasis in the PRESENT. You can do something about the 'here and now'.

You are *MORE* likely to feel anxious when you think:	You are *LESS* likely to feel anxious when you think:	Tick (✓) the thinking approaches you will now take:
• about the PAST	about the PRESENT, here and now	
• about the FUTURE, especially the long-term future	about here and now, about the VERY NEXT THING YOU DO	
• NEGATIVE self-statements	POSITIVE self-statements	
• about YOURSELF	about TASKS: things you can achieve today	
• about WIDER or LARGER issues, concerns or tasks	about SPECIFIC issues, concerns or tasks	
• of SATISFYING others, e.g. what other people will say	of SATISFYING yourself	
• about things YOU CANNOT DIRECTLY AFFECT even if you try	about things YOU CAN DIRECTLY AFFECT if you try	
• that you are UNABLE TO STOP YOURSELF THINK-ING ABOUT A CONCERN	that you are ABLE TO STOP YOURSELF THINKING ABOUT A PARTICULAR CONCERN	
• you are UNPREPARED	you are PREPARED	
• POSTPONE thinking or doing anything	you are going to take IMMEDIATE APPROPRIATE ACTION	

Fig. 13. Stress reduction checklist.

- Thinking about the long-term future can often feel daunting, even overwhelming. Thinking 'What would happen to me if I fail' fuels anxiety and is counter-productive to success. Planning the short-term future, the VERY NEXT THING YOU DO, the next 15 minutes, hour, evening, day, week, provides a useful manageable structure.

- Thinking about yourself: how you are feeling, how worried you are, your health, your career prospects, is one of the commonest forms of self-produced stress when studying. The need, when revising for and taking exams, is for you to be able to focus yourself effectively on TASKS, particularly those that are manageable and can be tackled immediately. Chapter 3 on **Organising Your Revision** is packed with suggestions as to how to do this effectively.

- The explanation for avoiding negative self-statements is contained in **Turning negative self-statements into positive self-statements** (pages 133–134).

- When you say to yourself, 'I must work tonight' or 'I've got to get some revision done', you are likely to feel overwhelmed. Being highly SPECIFIC about issues, concerns or tasks gives you a manageable routine of activities. An example of an appropriate specific self-statement would be: 'I am going to make a revision card on topic X, test myself on it during the next 30 minutes or so. I'll then make myself a drink and listen to a CD before I tackle the next topic Y in the same way.'

- Even though we can often be more demanding of ourselves than others would be, it is generally more stressful to be thinking about what others expect of you, what they would say if you didn't get the grades or failed, etc. Fear of letting others down is a common form of exam anxiety and an enormous waste of emotional energy. SATISFYING YOURSELF and your own standards is a productive use of your energy.

- You cannot directly affect the examination system, the form it takes, the efficiency or justice of it or when you will take your examinations. Thinking about these is likely to leave you feeling out of control and relatively powerless. You can DIRECTLY AFFECT dozens of things about your life and study – this book is packed with suggestions of what and how – and these are going to help you feel more powerful and resourceful.

- If you are unable to stop yourself thinking about a concern it will certainly fuel your stress. You are ABLE TO STOP YOURSELF THINKING ABOUT A PARTICULAR CONCERN. Use **Turning negative self-statements into positive self-statements** (below) as well as these guidance notes to aid this process.

- If you are unprepared – don't know how to revise, have few stress coping techniques and don't know much about the examination procedure – you are certainly more likely to be stressed. You are doing something positive to be PREPARED by reading and using parts of this book.

- Postponing thinking about or doing something invariably fuels anxiety, increasing the intensity, occupying emotional energy unproductively. Taking IMMEDIATE APPROPRIATE ACTION like you are now by using this book is going to relieve these feelings.

Stopping negative thoughts
If you are having thoughts that worry you, try to say consistently to yourself 'Stop' – you may wish to choose another *command word* that has more meaning to you, e.g. your surname 'Acres!' or something positive 'Think positive' – as soon as you are aware of beginning to think or feel in a particular way. You can add to this some physical movement, like a click of your fingers to reinforce this command to yourself. You must be totally consistent if you adopt this approach. It may be hard work for the first day or so, but after that it will become a habit. This technique is usefully combined with **Turning negative self-statements into positive self-statements** (below), i.e. saying 'Stop' to yourself is followed by some positive statement about yourself, your intentions or your success to date.

You can see the usefulness of thought stopping when you feel panic coming on. It is demonstrated in **Coping with panic in an emergency** (page 149).

Turning negative self-statements into positive self-statements
Stress is often maintained by identifiable negative self-statements. Below in the left-hand column are examples of negative self-statements. In the right-hand column are examples of positive self-statements designed to replace them. Try to identify your own negative self-statements and write them in the blank spaces in the left-hand column. Then, using the positive examples above as a guideline, construct your own positive self-statements. Abandon all negative self-statements and put your energy into positive self-statements.

NEGATIVE STATEMENTS	POSITIVE STATEMENTS
I can't concentrate.	My concentration has really improved. Even when it lapses I know how to recover it.
I can't cope.	I can cope and I'm going to do so.
Everyone seems to be doing more work than I am.	Other people are irrelevant – it's the quality of my learning that matters and I now have the techniques to do my work well.
I might fail. I am going to fail. What if I fail . . .? I won't be able to face 'X' again . . .	I intend to pass, I'm doing a lot to ensure that happens and I can only do my best. That's what I intend to do.
I'm in a mess with my revision. I'll never be able to do enough or catch up. I don't know where to start.	I can get my work done in time when I plan a proper *revision timetable, decide priorities* and know *how to revise* efficiently.
I always make a mess of exams. I've never been able to do well at exams.	The past is irrelevant. I'm now working well and have learnt the techniques to do well in these exams — a new beginning.

Managing exam nerves: self-statements to help you cope

One way of managing your 'nerves', that is your anxiety or even panic, is to learn by heart some statements to help you cope. In the following four situations choose those statements which you can say convincingly to yourself either silently or out loud. At first, you may find it difficult to say any statement convincingly to yourself. In which case, follow this sequence:

- Choose one of two from the existing list *or* add your own.

- Make the statement *real* and realistic to you. Alter it so it remains positive but feels like something you could say to yourself.

- Practise saying it to yourself, regularly. You are aiming for it to become a well-ingrained habit to say these statements to yourself rather than the old negative, worrying statements.

- Once you have mastered one or two, add others, expanding your list of useful self-statements, following the same system as above.

Making the self-statements
Other action you can take is in brackets.

1. Preparing for my exams
What is it I have to do? (Extract all the parts for you from the examination techniques and anxiety coping sections of this book.)
I'm going to plan what to do about my anxiety and not waste time being anxious.
I'm going to think positively – no negative self-statements. (See other ideas in **Reducing stressful thinking**, page 130.)
I'm not going to get involved in conversations I don't want. (Keep conversations that may be anxiety-provoking brief and manageable.)
I'm going to be ready for anything that happens to me.
If the worst happens I'm not going to be thrown into a panic – I'll learn how to cope. (See, for example, **Coping with panic in an emergency** (page 149).
It will be different this time, I know how to cope.

2. During the exam itself
Now's my chance to put into action what I've learned.
Stick to the here-and-now.
What is the very next thing I'm going to do?
It's different this time – I know how to cope.
I can handle me *and* the tasks.
I can reason and/or relax my fear away.
I need some anxiety: I'll make what I feel work *for* me. (You do! It's a stimulus to coping, awareness, etc.)
Relax, I'm in control. Take a slow, deep breath.
Great. This gives me the chance to show what I know, think, believe, understand, can do, etc.

3. Coping with the feeling of being overwhelmed
Stop! I can manage this panic: it's no different from any other situation – use the exercises!
When fear comes, just pause.
Stick to here-and-now: What is the very next thing I'm going to do?
I could expect my fear to rise at times. Don't try to eliminate the fear, just keep it manageable.
Label my fear from 0 to 10 and watch it change.

4. Looking back on the experience
What an achievement.
There'll always be something I could have done better but I've really done well.

It's a great feeling.

I'm really making progress.

I managed my fear.

It wasn't as bad as I expected.

I've done it.

Wait until I tell . . . (fill in the name of someone important you'd really want to tell.)

Quoting to yourself

Finding a quotation or saying can be another form of self-statement you can use to prepare yourself and maintain your composure.

Example

This is one of my favourite quotes, a Sanskrit saying which I hear at the end of yoga classes.

> May you rise in tranquillity
> walk in peace and
> stay in harmony.

It creates in me a feeling of calm and well-being.

There are many others from which you can derive pleasure and good feelings. If you can find a quotation which helps you have a helpful perspective on life and exams, keep it with you, or pin it up in front of you where you study.

It is particularly helpful to find a phrase which helps you reaffirm a sense of yourself and a sense of well being. Said to yourself in a moment of potential or real stress, it can stop any feelings of overwhelmedness. I have known students change their perception of exams expressing complete surprise at being able to look forward to a group of exams, instead of being very frightened of them. There are other ideas in this section, particularly concerned with visualising and using all your senses, which can help you change your perceptions around too.

COPING WITH STRESSFUL SITUATIONS

How you think, feel or behave can be reinforced by being back in the same immediate environment, in the same place or same situation, e.g. being in the same room, house, library or with the same people around you.

Here are approaches you can take to cope with stress related to situations.

- *For situations that cannot be avoided* and yet cause you to feel stressed, learn and practise the relaxation ideas in this section. You can come to feel better feelings about people and places by adopting a calmer, more positive, more relaxed approach.

Where your anxiety is related to unknown or unfamiliar situations, e.g. the exam room, then try to simulate the situation as closely as possible, e.g. if your anxiety is about where you are going to take the exam, then find the room in advance, enter it when you are able to do so, get the feel of being in it in a quiet atmosphere. (See also **Getting used to exams**, page 101.)

- *Avoid those situations that cause you stress and that are avoidable.* Identify the situations you find stressful. You may wish to list them below or on a separate sheet of paper.

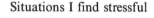

Situations I find stressful

Once identified you may wish to use a helper to talk over what you could do to avoid or minimise the stress involved in these situations. Tackling the problem may also be a useful aid.

- *Alter what you are doing in these situations* to minimise the stress. For example, if where you are revising is causing you stress, you may be able to improve the furniture arrangement. Moving a piece of furniture so that you get a better view, more natural daylight or enough heat is one approach. Arranging books, files, papers, pens and equipment so that they are accessible around you would be another approach.

- Make a point of *placing yourself in those situations that make you feel good*, relaxed, purposeful, as often as you are able to do so. You may wish to list them below or on a separate sheet of paper. See also **Finding a retreat or sanctuary** (pages 138–139).

Situations in which I feel good

- *Vary* where you are and who you are with to give yourself the stimulus of a change in environment. Although establishing an effective routine can help both to complete tasks and to work in a composed and effective manner, it may at times leave you feeling unstimulated, bored, jaded.

- *Balancing* a day, or a week or a weekend between tasks, places, people, work, recreation, exercise, diet, sleep and entertainment is a very important skill in maximising the effectiveness of your study.

Finding a retreat or sanctuary

A retreat may be outdoors or inside a building. It is a place that feels quiet and where even if there is noise it does not disturb or affect your stillness or focus. In this place you can compose yourself and feel composed.

It may be an actual place such as an old barn in the countryside or the side of a stream which flows into the sea – two real examples of people's sanctuaries. It may be inside a building such as the corner of a public library. The place may not even be quiet. I started to write this idea on a train journey and wrote 'it feels like a quiet place even though there are the sounds of people and the train's movement . . .' I am completing this writing in a college study bedroom listening to Mozart on a Walkman whilst attending a conference. This too feels like a sanctuary even though it's a strange room in a previously unknown place.

In other words, you can carry around your sanctuary with you. Even in unfamiliar places you can organise your environment by sitting at a desk with papers organised around you, your favourite pen in your hand, and perhaps listening to music which soothes and aids your concentration.

You can also organise your inner world as well as your immediate environment. You can take yourself inside yourself to be in touch with feelings of composure experienced elsewhere. There is also the opportunity to *create a scene in the imagination* which may not bear any resemblance to an actual place but which will produce powerful feelings of well being.

Calming yourself simply and quickly

From this collection of ideas to help you achieve calm, in different situations and different times, you can select the ideas that suit you – or create your own.

- Waste time by doing something which has no importance in relation to your study. Take the pressure off yourself.

- Do something meaningless and repetitive, e.g. arranging pebbles in a pile, shuffling cards.

- Avoid highly stressed people (or at least severely restrict the time you spend with them).

- Notice your breathing – enjoy the simple process of breathing in and out.

- Pause between tasks. Don't immediately follow the completion of one task by starting another. Give yourself a moment to enjoy the achievement and prepare yourself for the next.

- Smile. Practise smiling in the mirror – even if you don't feel like it.

- Look out for beautiful things such as a lovely sky, a beautiful flower or a favourite picture.

- Soak your face in warm water.

- Smell lavender. Pick some and keep it in your pocket.

- Go somewhere quiet for 30 seconds to break the pattern.

- Walk in an open space such as park, a field or a beach.

- Buy an ioniser and use it in a room you use for studying. Ionisers affect the balance between positive and negative ions. They claim to have an effect similar to the after-effect of a thunderstorm: the air feels clearer and fresher. This may be particularly helpful for you if you
  – have a sensitivity to a room's atmosphere

– are sensitive to dust particles in the air
– suffer from respiratory problems.

- Laugh. Find somebody who makes you laugh; watch a favourite video; read or listen to something you know amuses you.

- Buy and use a drop or so of Rescue Remedy from a chemist or health-food shop. A drop or two on your tongue may help you as a calming technique.

You will find other ideas in Paul Wilson's books, and others (see **Further Reading**).

COPING WITH KEY TIMES

Waking up in the morning
There are times during revision when you can feel jaded when waking. Apart from washing and showering, these ideas may help.

Putting your best feet forward
When the ideas of a *Paddle in cold water* and a *Bare foot walk* appeared in the first edition of this book, they received much media attention of the 'Ho . . . Ho . . . Ho . . .' variety. An international news agency in San Diego phoned this loony in England who had this weird idea. These are the two ideas, repeated as in the original.

Paddling in cold water. Walking up and down in 1 or 2 inches of water in a bath for a minute to two. Not as painful as a cold shower but refreshing, stimulating!

Walking in bare feet. Walk in bare feet on paving stones or grass, even with the dew rising, for a few minutes. Walk slowly, steadily, feeling the ground under your feet. This is refreshing and stimulating.

Their principles are simple. Water is a reviver. If you are tired, cold water is likely to revive you. For years, I have used this principle to run some cold water from the shower head onto my feet before it warms up to the temperature I want my shower to be. It helps to wake me up.

And half the world's population start their day in bare feet, walking on the bare earth – whether by choice or not. There is real advantage in bare feet for 'earthing' or 'grounding' yourself and setting yourself up for the new day. It is not always possible or desirable to do it in colder climates – it is not the top of everyone's preferences on cold winter mornings in Britain! It fits better in the summer.

Exercising physically
A jog, run, brisk walk or swim are all potentially stimulating at the

beginning of a day. Your circulation can equally well be stimulated by stepping up on a chair, and stepping down again, between 5 and 10 times, or any similar exercises, such as those contained in the Canadian Air Forces XBX exercises. All these physical pursuits need to be appropriate to your health, fitness and age to aid your alertness rather than decrease it!

Breathing
'The complete breath' is a version of the simple yoga exercise, described in Richard Hittleman's useful book, *Yoga for Health*. It is included in **Breathing effectively** (pages 149–152).

Drinking water
One simple technique for picking up your energy level is to drink water. If your energy feels low, pause, sit still and sip some water until you feel 'revived' to tackle the next stage of your learning.

There is a tendency among many students to drink too little water during periods of intense study. Hot stimulant drinks such as coffee do not have the same benefit as pure water, although they may raise your adrenalin in a different way.

Preparing on the morning before an afternoon exam

- Prepare a free morning before an afternoon exam in advance. By the evening before, know how you are going to spend the time, dividing it into half-hour and, if appropriate, quarter-hour units.

- Plan into the morning some relaxation, exercise or quiet; low key entertainment, e.g. listening to music.

- *Don't attempt any new revision topics* – Attempting to learn *new* topics at this late stage can affect your recall of those topics you already know and/or understand well.

- Use any key word cards or notes you have, not great bulky files, simply to recall and re-check your understanding, asking questions to which you will provide answers, without looking at the card. This simulates the exam conditions.

- For a paper involving mathematics or problem-solving, practise your recall of methods or formulae for more familiar questions.

- Plan into the morning when and what you are going to eat and drink. Try to eat something of nutritional value, but watch your liquid intake – many exams are 2 or 3 hours long!

- Incorporate all the relevant ideas from **Making your way to the exam** (page 142).

Making your way to the exam

You will maximise your effectiveness in examinations if you organise the time immediately before an examination. It will also enable you to minimise your anxiety. Some or all of the following ideas will also help.

- Minimise your waiting time outside an exam room, know the location of the room and time your walk, rehearsing it if necessary. You may either come direct from your home or find a temporary waiting place near the exam room that you can use until a few minutes before the examination.

- Meet only those people you want to meet, if any. Agree with friends not to stand around before the exam making anxiety-provoking conversation, e.g. about how nervous you are feeling, what topics you have revised or questions you think are going to be on the paper. Avoid waiting around outside altogether or talking to anybody, if you wish, by timing your arrival so that you can walk straight into the room a few minutes before the exam is due to start.

- Practise your rehearsed self-statements. Keep them positive. You are ready to go.

- Practise your breathing, visualising, muscular and/or **Coping with panic in an emergency** (page 149) techniques both to keep your composure and as practice in the event of their being needed.

GETTING TO SLEEP AT NIGHT

If you are finding it hard to fall asleep at night or are waking early, there are several approaches you can take. Select those which have most appeal to you, are most available and possible.

Usefully lying awake

A first approach is to cope with any anxiety you are feeling about the disrupted sleep pattern. You can almost certainly lose sleep for short periods of time without the loss having a profound effect upon you. You can exaggerate the importance of getting to sleep and occupy yourself with unnecessary worry about lying awake at night.

There's nothing wrong with lying awake at night. You can make it useful to you by:

- Enjoying and relaxing in your wakefulness and savouring the physical comfort of your bed.

- Enjoying some time of solitude, some time to yourself without having to communicate with other people.

- Having some time to think over things you often have little time to reflect upon.

- Writing down some of your thoughts, ideas, remembered information. Keeping a pad and pencil/pen by your bedside will help you:
  – capture good ideas
  – recall the things you have learned
  – list things you want or need to do in the next day or week
  – note and express the things you may be worrying about
  – keep up your **learning journal** (page 31).

- Practising relaxation approaches such as the **corpse** (pages 147–148) or **Breathing slowly and deeply** (page 150).

You may, of course, be deliberately cutting down on sleep to cram in more revision and study time. You can keep a check on whether this sleep loss is adversely affecting your study effectiveness by self-monitoring. Ask yourself:

- Are you being agitated, upset or angered by small incidents?
- Is your concentration noticeably deteriorating, both by 'not being able to take anything in' or not being able to recall something you have just read or done?
- Are you feeling emotionally overwhelmed by all the tasks?
- Do you lack energy and/or appetite?

If the answer to some of these questions is 'yes', then it is likely that your need for sleep (or proper diet, exercise, company, entertainment or relaxation, which are also considered in this section of the book) is not being met.

Getting to sleep checklist

Watching what you eat
Don't eat too late at night, particularly more indigestible foods. Give your body time to digest whatever you have eaten.

Watching what you drink
Apart from taking in too much liquid which could disturb your sleep by the pressure on your bladder, you will want to minimise your use of stimulants in the one-and-a-half hours before you want to sleep.
   Stimulant drinks include tea, coffee, cocoa, cola drinks, hot chocolate and alcohol. Alcohol needs to be monitored: whilst a small

quantity can act as a relaxant and decrease your alertness, larger quantities will act as a depressant and reduce your ability to rest easily.

You may find hot milk, Horlicks or camomile tea helps you go to sleep.

Using a comfortable bed
Check that your bed – including your pillow(s) is comfortable and that the area of your bed is just as you wish it to be in order for you to enjoy the prospect of lying down and going to sleep in it.

Organising your bedroom
If your bedroom is a study-bedroom, then ensure you have a distinct area of the room that you clear for sleep. You want to be able to associate that area of the room, when it is arranged to your satisfaction, with a good night's sleep.

Check to see if lying in bed studying, watching TV or listening to music help you sleep. If you are having trouble sleeping, train yourself to use the bed solely for sleeping.

Keep the bedroom temperature below 20°C (70°F) – if it is too warm it may disturb your sleep.

Using relaxing oils
You can place a few drops of fragrant oil on a handkerchief or tissues and place them under your pillow.You could also burn fragrances such as lavender during the day in an oil burner in your bedroom. Ask at a shop which sells aromatherapy products for guidance.

Taking exercise
Walks, jogs, runs, swims, a game of squash, an exercise programme, are all familiar, appropriate examples. Being physically tired, even exhausted, does certainly help you sleep. Studying is often a very physically passive business: it needs to be broken up with activity and a change of scenery.

Experiencing a sense of achievement
If you have completed a task, no matter how small, you are likely to be able to rest easier. Use the techniques in Chapter 3, **Organising your revision** to help with this.

Learning to juggle
Juggling has become particularly popular as a way of relaxing over the last few years. There is a school of thought which says that in order to manage the stress and strains of study, everyone can do something 'mindless' for five minutes every day, that is, something which requires

no conscious thought. Juggling is a very good example of a meditative technique which becomes relaxing as you begin to develop a little confidence and competence in it.

Exercising and using postures
Use relaxation exercises or postures, illustrated and explained in this book. Practise them working at a good, relaxed, sleeping posture. See **Developing a good sleeping posture** (pages 146–147).

Recalling the day – in reverse
When in a relaxed sleep posture, try, as an alternative to counting sheep, recalling the events of the day moment-by-moment in detail. However, do it backwards, i.e. starting from the very last thing you did before you got into bed. Hopefully you won't get as far as recalling when you woke up.

Meeting your need for entertainment
Meet your need for entertainment, for a break from study. Think about what causes you to enjoy yourself, relax and take your mind fully away from study. The list of possible activities is endless. The following are some examples students have mentioned to me during the course of one term: playing a guitar, listening to music on headphones, writing songs and poems, watching films, taking photographs, going to discos, going to the pub, cooking a meal for friends.

Enjoying the close company of others
A close friendship or friendships, involving the ability to share intimacies, be open, be yourself, is immensely valuable at any time and particularly at times of pressure.

Using water
Water is very therapeutic. Warm baths or showers can be excellent relaxants immediately before going to bed. Swimming may also help but is also, for some, a way of energising themselves.

Taking saunas and massage
If you have access to a sauna or know anybody who can offer a skilled massage, both are excellent relaxants prior to sleep.

Going to bed at a time you are ready for sleep
You may be familiar with the idea of 'biological clocks', that everybody has a natural rhythm, a sequence of ups and downs (cycles) that affect their alertness, need for sleep, mood and other

aspects of their being. Whether or not you understand or accept the idea, there seems to me to be no doubt that there are differences in both the amount of sleep people need and the time they need to go to sleep.

Some people need to get to bed early after completing their study in the early evening, whilst others can work very effectively late at night, studying to midnight and beyond. In general, those in early or mid-teens seem less able to study late into the night than those in late teens or older age groups, but there will be exceptions. If you have developed an effective means of self-monitoring yourself, you can prevent yourself from attempting to work beyond your productive limits. Try to be honest with yourself. If you know it is your anxiety that is keeping you up and your concentration, understanding and retention are poor, you are wasting time that could be valuably used the next day for study.

Likewise, there is no point in going to bed to try to sleep when you don't feel like sleep. Use the time more constructively, more creatively (as suggested above). Further, there seems little point in lying in bed worrying about not sleeping. You would be better occupied doing something which caused you less stress: making yourself a drink; listening to music on headphones; tackling a small, yet niggling, study task; using one of the relaxation exercises.

Finding someone to talk to
Seek out those people to whom you can talk with confidence. Those who will listen attentively, not moralise, keep confidentiality and help you to put things in perspective. Take this book along. Use it together, selecting the ideas which best suit you.

And if you still aren't sleeping . . .
If your lack of sleep continues it may be advisable to visit your doctor. There is no clear-cut guideline on how long you should tolerate disruption of sleep before seeking help, although between one and three weeks would seem appropriate.

Developing a good sleeping posture
A good sleeping posture is illustrated in Figure 14. Lie on your right side, drawing up your bent left leg so that it comes comfortably to rest alongside your waist area. Your right leg stretches out straight.

Allow your right arm to lie straight alongside your right side, whilst your left arm is bent. Your head should be supported by a pillow or pillows.

You may prefer to try this on your left side or make small alterations to the position of your arms and legs.

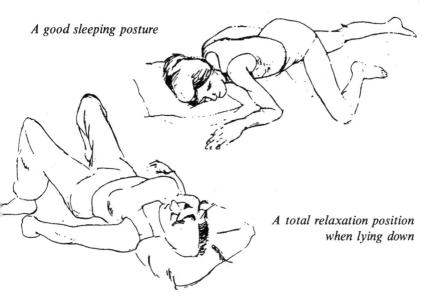

A good sleeping posture

*A total relaxation position
when lying down*

Fig. 14. Sleeping and relaxation positions.

The corpse

The objective of the 'corpse' is to be able to completely relax every muscle in your face and body. Anxiety will lessen when you relax muscles.

It involves lying on the floor, a bed, in or on a sleeping bag, pillows or cushions and is a position that encourages deep relaxation and sleep. Wear comfortable, loose clothing and dispense with shoes.

- Lie down slowly on your back with your arms by your sides.

- Allow your arms to come to rest with your hands a few inches away from your body and palms upwards, curling your fingers if they want to do so.

- Your feet should be allowed to fall open, spreading outwards, until they settle in a comfortable position a few inches apart.

- Raise your chin 6 to 8 cm (2 inches or so), tilting your head backwards so that your eyes are looking directly above you, then close your eyes.

- Try to let all your muscles become limp and heavy. Let your facial muscles go, your arms and legs become floppy and heavy, settling into a comfortable, still posture.

- Inhale deeply and slowly to enable your whole breathing to slow down with each intake of breath, don't take another breath until you have to do so. Simply concentrate your attention on your breathing and nothing else.

- You may stay in this position for any length of time. When you have finished, rise very slowly to avoid dizziness, raising yourself into a sitting or semi-upright position on your right side before eventually standing.

A total relaxation position when lying down

Initially, lie as in the position for the 'corpse There are two differences as you can see in Figure 14. The first is that you raise your knees, so that they are firmly and comfortably supported by your feet on the ground. The knees should be between approximately 12 cm and 30 cm (6 to 12 inches) apart.

The second difference is that you raise your head 5 to 8 cm (2 to 3 inches) by resting the back on a thick book or books or a cushion. As with the corpse, raise your chin by tilting your head back 5 cm (2 inches) or so.

You may then close your eyes, breathing slowly and deeply as in the corpse.

As with the corpse, you may continue in the position which enables the base of your spine to be very comfortably supported, as long as you wish or time permits. Rise, as in all such exercises, very slowly, sitting up first then slowly rising to your feet.

This is a lovely relaxing position, for a few minutes or a longer period of time.

Closing your eyes – the cat nap

Closing your eyes for a few minutes can be extremely valuable at times of pressure. Twenty minutes sleep, lying down, sitting on a comfortable chair or sofa, can be immensely refreshing and enable you to continue your studying for some hours afterwards.

Example

My own favourite is to use the corpse, lying on the floor or on my bed. I set an alarm clock if I know I do not want to over-sleep but I generally find I stir naturally, using my own time clock. I do not necessarily fall into a deep sleep, but I am conscious of cutting off from full consciousness and enjoying the experience of relaxing physically, as well as emotionally.

BREATHING EFFECTIVELY

Learning how to breathe more fully and appropriately by using one or more of these exercises is another very helpful approach to removing tension and refreshing yourself.

Coping with panic in an emergency

This exercise is to counteract panic and the build-up of tension. It is adapted from Jane Madder's useful book *Stress and Relaxation*.

1. Say sharply to yourself STOP! (aloud if the situation permits).
2. Breathe in and hold your breath for a moment before *slowly* exhaling. As you do so relax your shoulders and hands by dropping them. (See also **A do-it-yourself guide to muscular relaxation**, Figure 16)
3. Pause for a moment, then as you breathe in slowly again, relax your forehead and jaw (allow them to drop a little).
4. Stay quiet for a few moments then go on with what you were doing, moving slowly and smoothly.
5. If you have to talk, speak a little more slowly and with your voice a little lower than usual.

This STOP! relaxation can usually be done without anybody noticing and you will find that, in spite of your feelings, the tension will lessen.

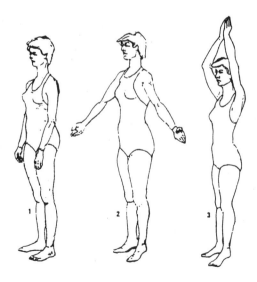

Fig. 15. Breathing exercises.

Taking the complete breath

The essential feature of this exercise is that everything is completed SLOWLY.

1. Stand upright with your arms by your side. Exhale (see Figure 15. 1).
2. Breathe in through your nose. As you do so, inhale, filling as fully as possible your stomach/abdomen area first and thereafter your chest (see Figure 15.2).
3. At the same time, bring your arms above your head and rise on to your toes.
    Hold this for a moment (see Figure 15.3).
4. Breathe out through your nose, expelling the air from your abdomen through your chest. As you do so, lower your arms to your sides and your feet to the floor again.

You can repeat this between 3 and 10 times. If you wish you can count to 8 as you inhale and do the same as you exhale. Alternatively, you can start to raise yourself onto the balls of your feet when your arms reach the horizontal halfway point of their journey to above your head, lowering yourself onto your heels slowly from the halfway point of their journey down.

Breathing slowly and deeply

The same sequence illustrated in **Taking the complete breath** (Figure 15) can be used at any time, without the accompanying stretching movements. It is useful to avoid the build-up of tension, or to reduce it once it has occurred. The sequence is as follows:

1. Breathe in slowly through your nose to the count of 8. As you inhale the air, imagine you are filling your stomach/abdomen area first and thereafter your chest.
2. Hold this breath in for as long as it remains comfortable to do so.
3. Expel the air slowly through your nose to the count of 8, expelling the air from your abdomen upwards through your chest.
4. Refrain from taking another intake of breath until it becomes uncomfortable and repeat the sequence 1 to 4, again.

Three times is usually enough to reduce the level of tension and to refresh you. You may extend this if you need to do so. It is a useful technique for the exam room.

Alternate nostril breathing

This is an effective relaxant that can help with tension and head congestion.

Inhale through the right nostril, closing the left nostril with the thumb of your left hand. Count slowly to 4 as you inhale.

Close both nostrils with your left thumb and forefinger and hold your breath to the slow count of 4.

Exhale through your left nostril to the slow count of 4, whilst closing your right nostril with your forefinger (or first two fingers whichever you find easier).

Release both nostrils, remaining without breath for another count of 4.

Repeat, breathing in through the left nostril.

Once you have established an even 4-4-4-4 routine and can complete the thumb and forefinger movements easily, close your eyes when doing this exercise.

You can try variations on this 4-4-4-4 routine. Try *in* for 6, count to 3; *out* for 6, count to 3; *in* for 6, etc. 8/4/8/4 combinations, once you're used to the others, will slow and deepen your breathing even more. You can practise this exercise for 5 minutes or so at a time – even three or four sequences will be beneficial.

Breathing at three levels

There are three levels of breathing which you can come to detect well if you practise yoga techniques.

Level one
When you are anxious your breathing is often shallow. If you locate where you are breathing it is at the top of the chest. You will probably find you are breathing quite quickly. If asked to speak your voice is likely to tremble and be quite quiet with this level of breathing.

Level two
This is deeper breathing which comes to and from the chest. You are likely to feel less anxious, have a stronger voice when asked to speak in a public situation and breathe more slowly than in level one. Much of your breathing in everyday life is likely to be in level two (or fluctuating between level one and level two).

Level three
When you take a full, deep, intake of breath you move into level three breathing. What happens is that your diaphragm moves down to create a vacuum in the lung cavity and pushes out the abdomen. You can see and feel your stomach filling up and emptying. You could imagine

yourself filling up a balloon on the in-breath. If you gently lay your hand on your stomach you will feel it rise and fall. The higher you go the better as it means that you are drawing in air to fill the lungs. Do not overstrain though.

Breathe through the nose whenever possible and breathe out through the nose as well.

Your out-breath should be more emphasised than the in-breath and take a little longer. If you sigh slightly as you release the breath, you will find it will help to release tension.

Similarly, if you tense and then relax your shoulders by allowing them to drop with a sigh, you will be helping to let go of your tension.

You can also hold your breath at the end of the exhalation, for 2 to 5 seconds, to enable yourself to be still before a full inhalation begins.

As with other exercises in breathing you need only repeat it five times in order to feel the benefit of this deep breathing exercise, which you can do in a sitting position. Over time it will generate a feeling of well being.

RELAXING YOUR MUSCLES

The basic principle involved in muscular relaxation is that when muscles are tensed really hard and then relaxed, the muscles will go into a deeper state of relaxation than formerly. When your muscles are relaxed in this way *you cannot be in a state of tension* – the two states are not compatible. In such a composed physical state you are going to be able to study more effectively, and be mentally alert with the negative effects of anxiety behind you.

You can achieve muscular relaxation as an after-effect from strenuous physical exertion such as running, squash, swimming, squat thrusts and team ball games. Such exertion will cause you to breathe more deeply and fully and this will also contribute to your more relaxed state afterwards. There are obvious differences in fitness and overall health that determine what exercise is appropriate to you; how much exercise; how often and for how long. A marathon run is not generally an appropriate starting point for most people!

Look out for guidance booklets in local sports and recreational facilities, doctors' surgeries, schools and colleges for suggestions for looking after yourself. If in doubt, consult medical opinion. There are plenty of courses in adult education and community centres for you to use during the exam period too.

In addition, the following exercises will give you practice in muscular relaxation:

- a do it yourself guide to muscular relaxation (Figure 16)
- exercising when sitting at a desk (page 157)

- relaxing your head and neck (page 157)
- sit and relax (below)
- being hugged and cuddled (pages 157–158)
- touching for well-being (pages 158–160).

Guiding yourself to muscular relaxation

Relaxation of individual muscle groups or the whole body is a skill which everyone can learn and which improves with practice. It is important to be able to recognise muscle tension and then to release this tension at will. It is only when this skill has been learned that the full benefits of muscular relaxation during anxious and stressful situations can be achieved.

The following programme involves tensing and then relaxing the main muscle groups of the body in turn. Ideally, each group should be tensed and the tension released three times in succession:

- first of all tensing the muscles as tightly as possible
- secondly with moderate tension
- finally with minimal tension.

It may help you to count to 5 slowly and silently on each of these three tensings. This helps us to recognise the muscle tension which is part of our reaction to stress, and the contrasting feel of muscles which are relaxed.

The best way to learn the skill of relaxation is to find a friend who will slowly talk you through the programme on pages 155–156. If this is not possible, read through the programme and learn the order of muscles to be relaxed and then work through from memory or from a key word card.

Time required
At first it will take approximately 20 to 30 minutes to go through the entire procedure properly. With practice you will be able to become quite relaxed in 10 to 15 minutes.

An alternative is to buy a commercially produced relaxation programme on audio-tape. Yet another alternative is to record your own audio-tape, using this programme.

Like any other skill (driving a car, playing the piano) it will need practice, but the benefits can be enormous, and it is enjoyable to do in itself!

Following the relaxation programme – some general guidelines
Sit and relax
Just settle back in a chair and find a position where you are

comfortable. Let the chair support your body weight. Let your hands rest on your lap and have your head comfortably balanced on your neck and shoulders. (If you prefer, lie down on the floor or on a bed with your legs stretched out. Let your arms lie loosely alongside your body, as in the 'corpse', palms turned down. If it is more comfortable have your hands resting across your abdomen.) Now close your eyes. Sigh to release tension. Pay attention to the rhythm of your own breathing. Breathe out a little more deeply. Feel your abdomen rise as you breathe in and as you exhale feel your whole body sink into the chair, letting all your muscles relax. Pause for a while.

You are now in a state of total relaxation
Concentrate on the rhythm of your own breathing as you sit/lie in total relaxation. Think of all the muscles you have just relaxed and feel them sinking into a deeper state of relaxation. In times of stress, muscle tension can manifest itself in different parts of the body – e.g. the

---

A Do It Yourself Guide to Muscular Relaxation
outline instructions for the programme in Figure 17

Sequence (Key word)   RELAXATION – Muscular

  1. Raise eyebrows   NB: *SLOWLY*

  2. Screw up eyes   Tensing – 3 times

  3. Clench teeth   Maximum)

  4. Ear-to-ear grin   Moderate) tensing to count

  5. Tongue   Minimum) of 5

         6. Wrist back – hand forward

         7. Bend elbows   *Note* Concentrate on most

         8. Hands and arms at side   stressed muscles.

  9. Chin out

10. Chin in

11. Neck stretch

12. Retract neck

13. Shrug shoulders

14. Shoulder blades

15. Arched back

         16. Pull in stomach   19. Point toes

         17. Heels against floor   20. Toes up

         18. Buttocks   21. Curl toes

Fig. 16. A guide to muscular relaxation.

Part of the body (key words)	Instructions (repeat each movement three times)	What you will feel (helpers read this aloud after the instructions)
Start with the face		Feel the tension across the forehead and scalp.
Forehead 1. Raise eyebrows	Raise your eyebrows and frown heavily, with maximum tension. *Repeat* with moderate and minimal tension.	Release the tension and feel the forehead become smooth and the muscles relax.
Eyes and nose 2. Screw up eyes	Screw your eyes up tightly.	Feel the tension spreading over the whole of your face and the contrasting calm, soothing feeling as the tension is released.
Mouth and jaw 3. Clench teeth	Clench your teeth together firmly to tense the jaw muscles.	Feel the tension around the jaw and throat. Release the tension and let your jaw muscles become loose letting your mouth hang open if it wishes.
4. Ear-to-ear grin	Tense the muscles around the mouth by smiling in an exaggerated way – an ear-to-ear grin – then let the smile fade away.	Feel the muscles relax.
5. Tongue	Tense the tongue by pressing it firmly against the back of the teeth. Slowly release and let the tongue rest in the mouth.	Feel the release of tension and the tongue relaxing in your mouth.
Forearms 6. Wrist back – hand forward	Bend your wrist back and push forward hard with your hand.	As you let the tension go, feel warm, tingling sensation of relaxed muscles in the forearms.
Upper arms 7. Bend elbows	Bend both arms at the elbow. Flex the biceps really firmly, slowly relax these muscles.	Feel the heaviness in your arms spread down to your finger tips.
Shoulders and chest 8. Hands and arms at side	Press your hands and the arms firmly against the side of your body. Press really hard and then release the tension and let your shoulders hang loose.	Your arms will feel heavy and relaxed again.

Fig. 17. Your relaxation programme.

Part of the body (key words)	Instructions (repeat each movement three times)	What you will feel (helpers read this aloud after the instructions)
Neck and back 9. Chin out	Jut your chin out in front of you or, if you are lying down, raise your head about one inch from the ground.	Feel the tension in your neck muscles and its release as you bring your head down to a comfortable resting position.
10. Chin in	Draw your chin in towards your neck or, if lying down, press your head back into the floor. Hold it briefly, then release.	Feel tension building in your neck, shoulders and back Enjoy the contrasting feel of the muscles as they relax and lose the tension.
11. Neck stretch	Elongate your neck and feel the tension until it is released.	Feel the tension until it is released and slowly subsides.
12. Retract neck	Retract your neck by shortening your neck as much as possible.	Feel the tension and slowly release it.
13. Shrug shoulders	Try and touch your ears with your shoulders then let them slump back.	Feel a heavy relaxed feeling once more which is spreading through your upper body.
14. Shoulder blades	Draw your shoulder blades firmly together.	Feel the tightness created then relax the muscles and let your shoulders slump.
15. Arched back	Hollow your back by arching it more and more. Relax back into chair or on to the floor.	Feel the support that the chair or floor offers.
Stomach, thighs and buttocks 16. Pull in stomach	Pull your stomach muscles in tighter and tighter, then let go.	Feel warmth and tingling feelings as it is released.
Heels against floor	With feet flat on the floor, pull the heels backwards against the resistance of the floor, tightening all the muscles at the back of the thighs. Relax these muscles. With feet still flat on the floor press the heels down firmly into the floor and let the muscles relax completely.	Feel the difference when the tension is released.
17. Buttocks	Tighten muscles in your buttocks and release.	Feel the release of tension that this produces.
Calves and feet 18. Point toes	Point your toes, extending the ankle joint. Then let the ankle become loose and the muscles relaxed.	Feel the tension in the muscles at the back of the lower leg.
19. Toes up	Flex the ankle by bending the toes up towards the knee.	Feel the tension build again. Feel the warm, tingling feeling of relaxation spread down your legs.
20. Curl toes	Curl your toes up tightly then release this tension 3 times.	With the strain release, let the toes rest naturally.
21. Stretch toes	Stretch your toes out strongly as far as you can.	As the feet relax completely let the soothing, heavy feeling in your legs spread to the tips of your toes.

clenched fist, the furrowed brow, the aching neck and shoulders – so *concentrate particularly on the muscle groups which reflect your anxiety and tension* and register the way they feel in this relaxed state.

Ending the relaxation programme
When you are ready to end this period of relaxation come round very slowly. Just wiggle your toes and fingers a little when you are ready, have a stretch and open your eyes. You should feel refreshed and calm, ready to face the demands of your daily life.

Exercising when sitting at a desk
These isometric exercises involve some of the same principles involved in **A do it yourself guide to muscular relaxation** (pages 154–156). You can try one or more of these exercises, in any order.

- Pull in stomach muscles tightly
  Hold for count of 5
  Relax

- Clench fist tightly
  Hold for count of 5
  Relax

- Extend fingers
  Hold for a count of 5
  Relax

- Grasp below seat of chair
  Pull up for count of 5
  Relax

- Press elbows tightly into side of body
  Hold for count of 5
  Relax

- Push foot hard into floor
  Hold for count of 5
  Relax

Relaxing your head and neck
Allow your head to DROP forward. Try not to pull it down. You should feel muscles at back of your neck being stretched by the weight of your head. Repeat, allowing your head to drop backward, then to the left and right.

A selection of the above exercises will only take about 30 seconds and can be most helpful to relieve the strain (or even cramp) which occurs when sitting writing at a desk during an examination. Performed between questions or sections of an exam, the exercises may also aid in 'switching off' from one topic and focusing on the next.

Being hugged and cuddled
In her *Little Book of Hugs*, Katherine Keating's cartoon bears point out the many and varied ways we can both give and receive a hug. Stressful times such as exams are times when we can be enormously supported by human touch and many students have said how

important a friend's cuddle or supportive arm around the shoulders has been when they have felt fragile and/or emotionally exhausted.

Visualising being hugged

Even if a safe hug is not available to you during the revision period (and it won't be in the exam room) then you can visualise receiving a hug.

Adopt the usual routine for calming and relaxing yourself by sitting in a comfortable, quiet place. Breathe slowly and deeply four or five times and allow yourself to sink into the chair, feeling the weight of your limbs.

Imagine yourself meeting a good friend, greeting each other with a 'hello' and a smile with you both putting your arms around each other in a gentle but firm, warm embrace. You can use this image for comfort and reassurance by practising it prior to the exams and using the image of it in the exam room if you're feeling the need of some support.

S-l-o-w-l-y does it

Another idea for calming yourself in the exam situation is to focus on the words SLOW and SLOWLY. Picture the word S L O W on a white or blackboard. Say it to yourself, slowly. Breathe in slowly, Hold your breath for a few moments and then let out the breath slowly.

When you slow your breathing down you slow your heart rate down too. You'll leave behind the shallow-breathing, heart-fluttering anxiety-state.

You can use this approach to help you read instructions on exam papers by saying S L O W and S L O W L Y to yourself as you first read, and then follow, the instructions precisely.

Touching for well-being

Here are three simple ideas you can use to help your own physical well-being.

1. Stroking your face

Using the fingertips of both hands, very lightly and gently stroke the surface of your face. Start with your forehead, laying your fingertips in the middle of your brow above your nose, and draw the fingers of both hands gently across your forehead at the same time. Do it slowly and repeat five times.

Then do the same, again using both hands very lightly
– over your eyes and eye sockets (5 times)
– along both sides of your nose, moving downwards (5 times)
– over the remainder of your cheeks, moving sideways (5 times)
– over your cheekbones, downwards to your chin (5 times)

– over your mouth and lips (5 times)
– under your cheek bone and along your neck (5 times)
– from your ears downwards (5 times).

You are likely to feel soothed as a result and the whole process only takes a few minutes.

2. Stroking forehead, arms and hands
Use one hand to gently stroke
– your forehead
– the inside of both arms where your elbow bends, ensuring you make skin-to-skin contact; use both hands to gently stroke both arms.
– use one hand to gently stroke the back of the other, then reverse it.

Do this slowly for as many times as you wish, and as often as you wish. (These three areas of the body have been found to provide maximum comfort to disturbed or upset children with special needs.)

3. Pressing on the palm
In the palm of your hand there is a spot which has been identified for thousands of years as being one of the meridians of the body and to be concerned with mental well-being.

It is located about four or five cms below the gap between our second and third fingers. If you feel around with your index finger into the opposite palm as it remains relaxed and facing upward, you will find a small indentation in your palm, into which your finger is able to press. If you have found the right indentation or dip in the hand, when you exert some pressure into that place it will feel a little sensitive, even sore. If it does, you have found the right place.

The idea is to exert some firm but gentle pressure with that one finger on that point, to stimulate a feeling of well-being. If you find that a far-fetched idea, you can also combine pressure with a visualisation of some pleasant scene or good experience. In that way you form a link between a discreet (quite well hidden) part of the body and another sensation you like (this is a process known as 'anchoring').

Students who had a fear of flying were able to use this technique successfully, combining it with a number of other anxiety management techniques contained in this chapter.

VISUALISING

Using visualisation in four ways

Creating a picture in your mind (visualisation) has at least four uses when studying for exams. Use the same upward eye movements as described in Chapter 4, **Improving your memory**.

1. Memorising

Its use has been explained in remembering and in constructing key word revision cards in Chapter 3, **Organising your Revision.**

2. Dreaming as a goal

Example

Duncan Goodhew, the British Olympic swimming champion (with his distinctive bald head), determined at the age of fourteen that he was going to swim in the Olympics. It was his target, his goal throughout the years of hard training. He imagined how the Olympic final would be; how the pool would be and how he would win the gold medal. He did this over and over again during the years before his success. His dream drove him on and sustained him through those years and the race itself was exactly as he had constantly pictured it.

This use of a dream as a goal is well known to many sportsmen and women. They are aware that it is not just ability, technique, determination or hard work that create success, but an extra key factor within the person. It is not always clear what this is, but a dream is certainly one such factor. Constructing your own dream, visualising what you intend to achieve for yourself, could become a powerful motivating force for you in your study.

3. Visualising taking the exam

Use one of the relaxation exercises to bring yourself into a composed, comfortable and relaxed state.

Now imagine yourself in the same composed, calm state taking the examination.

You feel purposeful and confident. You see yourself at a desk, in the exam room environment. You feel entirely at home and attuned to that moment, working effectively and concentrating well.

Practise visualising this positive, clear, realistic image over and over again.

4. Visualising as a relaxation technique
There are a number of ways of using visualisation to relax. A few examples follow on pages 161–163.

Creating a scene in your imagination
The ability to create a scene in your imagination as a place to retreat into when stress is near can be very useful.

- Think of a scene or a moment in time in your mind. It can be real or imaginary; from the past, present or future.

- The essential features of this scene are that it creates within you pleasant feelings of safety, warmth, security, peace.

- It must be unaffected by bad messages, uneasy thoughts, painful memories.

- In your imagination create as vivid a scene as possible. Picture the scene, the colours, the movement in the scene, the precise detail. *Hear* the sounds associated with the scene in the same kind of detail. *Feel* the touch experiences associated with the moment such as temperature, wind, the feel of your body, anything you touched. Add to these any *tastes* or *smells* associated with the moment.

- It may take you a little time to construct such a scene. You may choose to have more than one. Practise recalling this scene several times when not feeling stressed. With practice it can be very quickly brought to mind. It can only take a few seconds, or at most a minute or two, to dwell in this lovely imagined world. You can then quickly return to present reality in a more composed state.

You can use this technique in any situation, e.g. an exam room, standing around waiting for something to happen. It is not visible to other people, except perhaps by the peaceful look on your face.

In learning it, however, you may find it helpful to sit in a comfortable chair or lie on a bed and use other relaxation exercises such as breathing or muscular relaxation before it.

Imagining three alternative scenes
You may wish to try to take yourself in your imagination through all

three of these scenes or one may well appeal to you more than others.

Scene 1 – Exploring the glade

You come upon a sunlit glade in a forest. Move around it long enough to choose the best spot for you to sit or lie in complete comfort. Here is tranquillity, peace and calm. Here you can hear the sound of buzzing insects, smell the scents of the grasses and wild flowers shimmering in the heat whilst you watch the sunlight pushing through the rustling leaves in the trees that are around you.

Scene 2 – Sitting by the stream

You are sitting by the side of a stream. The spot you have chosen enables you to sit comfortably, perhaps hugging your knees, and to watch the stream as it rushes, glides and sparkles past you. You watch the progress of leaves as they whirl by or glide into the stiller waters at the edge of the stream. The sounds of the stream are constantly ringing in your ears and being absorbed into your being. You are aware of the lightest breeze touching your face. Here you can absorb yourself into being at one with the stream of life and the feeling of well-being.

Scene 3 – Lying on the beach

You are lying on a beautiful beach of golden sand. Ahead of you lies the deep blue ocean with its waves lapping against the sand. Behind and to the side you can see palm trees waving in the cooling breeze. The sky is cloudless and the sun beams down. You are warm, relaxed and full of well-being. All is well with your world.

With each of these scenes, count yourself out from them by simply saying '5-4-3-2-1' to yourself and then checking you are focused on the reality around you but with a composed frame of mind. You may not be able to use any of these three scenes because they fail to appeal to you or because you suffer from hay fever or have a concern about being near water or exposed to the sun. If this is the case, you can *create your own scene in your imagination.*

Relaxing with a wave of colour

- Sit comfortably in a chair or lie in a comfortable position.

- Close your eyes and imagine yourself to be transparent and filled with your favourite colour of liquid. Imagine it to be exactly at the temperature you find comfortable. If you are unsure of a colour, choose some variation of blue, e.g. turquoise or aquamarine.

- Starting from the crown of your head, imagine this liquid draining slowly away down your body. As it does so, imagine each part of the body from which it has drained feeling lighter and relieved of tension. Imagine the liquid eventually flowing out through the tips of your fingers and toes and you'll be left feeling relaxed. Repeat if necessary. Move only slowly when you first rise, to avoid dizziness.

Imagining your limbs feeling warm and heavy

Once you are aware of how muscles feel when they are relaxed and you have used your imagination to develop a composed state of mind, you can combine these two approaches in this exercise.

Lying down or sitting comfortably, imagine your limbs to be feeling very heavy. It may help you to close your eyes for a while and focus upon one part of the body at a time, e.g. your right hand; lower arm; upper arm.

Once all the limbs feel heavy, imagine a feeling of warmth in all these limbs. Exclude from this your neck area (where tension is often to be found). Imagine your neck to feel cool and light.

With practice this exercise only takes a few minutes and can be used in an upright sitting posture in the exam room.

Gazing as relaxation

A simple meditative exercise involves gazing at a *candle flame*. Light a candle and sit a distance of three to five feet or so away from it. Gaze into the heart of it – to the area just above the wick where there appears to be a vacuum in the flame. Minimise the amount of times you blink and two or three minutes of gazing is quite sufficient before you close your eyes. You may well see an after-image of the flame which you can follow behind your eyelids.

Ensuring that you are sitting in a comfortable chair, on a cushion or cross-legged on the floor, you will find this exercise will enhance your concentration and still your mind. You can add to it by playing some baroque music such as Mozart or some of the alternative types of music available from specialist shops and designed as meditative, whole earth or spiritual sounds.

Gazing at *movement in water* is another major way in which many people relax. Apart from gazing at waves crashing against the seashore or rushing over rocks in a stream, you will find that a number of waiting areas of doctors' and dentists' practices use another therapeutic device – the fish tank.

I have known very distressed people become calm within half an hour of gazing at small fish moving in a *tropical fish tank*. It is a well-known and successful way of shedding preoccupations, so if you have an opportunity to gaze at one – try it.

Listening in focus

This exercise complements the **Visualising taking the exam** (pages 160–161) exercise in that it helps focus attention and concentration in the exam room. In addition, it is a relaxation exercise in its own right. The object of the exercise is to develop your ability to listen to only those sounds you wish to hear and thus be more discriminating in your listening. Thus if potentially disruptive sounds occur in or outside the exam room you will continue to maintain your concentration. A window cleaner whistling; a lawn mower working outside (quite a common occurrence in summer exams); building or road works; another candidate taken ill are examples of situations that you will be able to take in your stride.

The exercise

- Spend around 60 seconds listening to sounds outside the room you are in, e.g. sounds of traffic, birds, rain or wind, voices, footsteps on stairs.

- Another 60 seconds listening to sounds in the room, e.g. a radiator clinking, the movement of a chair, a clock ticking, a cough.

- Another 60 seconds listening to the sounds immediately around you and within you e.g. breathing, the movement of your paper and pen, the sound of clearing your throat, your chair.

It is this third – emphasised – listening that you wish to be able to develop and use in the exam room, excluding the sounds in the room and beyond.

Practise being able to focus on your immediate environment in this way as an aid to your concentration.

FINDING OTHER APPROACHES

Booking to see a counsellor

You will probably be able to book an appointment to see a counsellor in most colleges of further and higher education. This will generally be a free service. Counselling has become a very heavily used service in post-school education. Some of the most experienced and effective helpers are to be found among counsellors, who will be available to work with your anxiety and any of the life circumstances that fuel it. You can find more information from the Association of University and College Counsellors (see **Useful Addresses**) and by asking in your local colleges and universities.

Seeking medical help

The whole of this book is devoted to strategies to help you cope with coursework and examinations by drawing on your own resources and those of your friends and relatives around you. However, there may be times when you feel so overwhelmed with anxiety that you feel permanently stressed and are exhibiting symptoms such as sickness, diarrhoea, loss of sleep and appetite. In such circumstances a visit to your doctor is highly appropriate.

Visiting your doctor

You may find someone with whom you can talk over how you are feeling and the symptoms you are experiencing. If your school, college or university does not have a counselling service, which hopefully it does, you may have the option of being referred to a practice counsellor or a psychologist to help you by talking through your concerns.

The doctor may also choose to prescribe some medication which is non-addictive. You may also have the choice of approaching a number of alternative practitioners.

Seeking alternative health approaches

There are many alternative medical approaches that can be of immense help to your management of anxiety. Among these would certainly be included acupuncture, aromatherapy (the use of aromatic oils in therapy) and reflexology. To find a safe and effective practitioner, consult the professional associations and listen out for personal recommendations from people whose opinions you trust.

Using homeopathic help

'Homeopathy offers a safe alternative as it treats the whole person – the physical as well as the emotional – and therefore plays an important role in the movement back to a more holistic approach to health' writes Miranda Castro in her book *The Complete Homeopathic Handbook*.

One of the remedies homeopaths may prescribe for exam problems is Argent Nitz. It will not be prescribed routinely; you will most probably have to be trembling with nervous excitement, suffering from diarrhoea and having impulsive thoughts tormenting you. The homeopath will take into account all the symptoms, the situation and you, before prescribing.

Details of how to find a homeopath near you are included in the **Useful Addresses** section at the back of the book.

Sucking a sweet. . .

Sucking a sweet or chewing gum is used by many candidates in the exam room. The easiest way to keep saliva in your mouth is to suck on a sweet. Glucose is particularly good and many students suck mints; checking with the college canteen on the morning of one exam, it was Polos that were the top seller.

The key point is to keep saliva in your mouth with or without a sweet. By keeping saliva in your mouth you are helping yourself to keep fears at bay.

. . . or carrying a talisman

The talis is an object to which luck, safety or wonderful things are linked. If you have a small object such as a pebble that you can carry with you and touch or rub or associate with well-being, it can be extremely helpful around exam times. You could use it in between and alongside revising sessions. You can also carry it with you on your journey to the exam room and have it with you in the examination room, placing it on your desk or keeping it in a pocket.

A friend gave me a piece of light green marble from Ireland which I use in this way. It had been beautifully smoothed into an oval shape with concave dips in each surface. The Irish call it a worry stone. I find it helpful to carry into new or stressful situations whether or not I look at it or touch its smooth surface. It acts as a source of reassurance and that is the essence of the idea of a talis.

You can create your own talis, even having more than one, in case one is mislaid.

7
Using Others as Helpers

NEGOTIATING HELP

This section gives guidelines to both students and their helpers (other students, friends, parents, spouses and others).

Throughout, it emphasises the importance of *negotiating help* with another person. That is, not demanding it or forcing it upon others but requesting and offering. In practical terms, this means that the helper asks questions like:

'Is there anything I can do to help?'

It also means that the student asks questions like:

'Could you help me with . . .?'

It also means that the answer to both these questions could be 'No', at least initially, and that the times and conditions for help have to be discussed. Helpers can state clearly what they are prepared to offer in the way of help. Students can state equally clearly their needs (when they know what they are); helpers can help them discover their needs where they are unclear.

Saying helpful and unhelpful things
I have asked students which things their parents, friends or other helpers say are most helpful and which are most unhelpful. They say:

Unhelpful   *Do you agree?*
It's not worth worrying about.
Cheer up.
Have you finished yet?
Pull yourself together.
You've just got to get down to it.

You must get down to it.
Get a grip on yourself.
Do some work and you'll feel better.
You can only do your best.
Don't worry.
It will be all right on the day.
Have your done your homework tonight?
Your brother/sister/cousin/friend, etc.
　　never had this problem . . .

Helpful　　　　　　　　　　　　　　　　*Do you agree?*
Is there anything I can do to help?
How's it going?
Do you want any help with anything?
How are you feeling about things?
Let me know if I can help in any way.
You seem to be working hard.
You are finding it difficult to get down to it.
I'll test you on that topic if you want.

Features of these comments and questions
They tend to be open questions, offering, without forcing, help. They accept the student's feelings.

You may find some items in the 'Unhelpful' list helpful and vice versa. It does not matter. It is important that you negotiate with your helper(s) so that they know what is helpful to you and what is not.

Working with students and friends
In the early days of schooling, you may often have felt as if you were cheating if you worked with other students on the same question. Working with others can be immensely useful, of course, and the following guidelines are designed to ensure the maximum usefulness.

- Work on each other's strengths, i.e. the topics you know best, are most interested in, etc.

- Constructively support each other by listening attentively; telling friends when they have been helpful; avoiding anxiety-provoking topics.

- Co-operate. Use any competitiveness to the benefit of all rather than the detriment of individuals. Don't try to elevate your own self-confidence at the expense of others (you will find fellow students who try this at exam time).

- Make group decisions binding on each member of the group. If you have voluntarily, without being placed under any duress, agreed to do something, you must answer to the group if you have not done so.

- Form groups to practise particular techniques, e.g. relaxation technique; visualisation for relaxation. Meet regularly and help each other.

Helping guidelines for all

- Work through the book yourself, familiarising yourself, in particular, with the parts that are of direct interest and concern to the student.

- Work through the book with the student, agreeing which parts apply.

- Try to avoid imposing your own anxieties on to the student when the student is feeling anxious. Discuss these *either* with another person *or* with the student when the student is less anxious and wants to listen *or* both.

- Don't expect the student to be working solidly through the revision and examination period because that would be an inefficient studying approach, as is explained in this book.

- Say clearly what you are prepared to offer in the way of help.

- The essence of helpful listening is that you are attentive and accept what the student says, without moralising or judging. By keeping their confidences to yourself, you enable them to express exactly how they feel, think and behave, without comparing them with others.

Helping guidelines for parents

Don Davies, author of *Maximising Examination Performance* (see **Further Reading** for details), gave these guidelines for parents in a newspaper feature on exam stress. Here they appear with some small amendments and some page references to parts of this book which give emphasis to his points or provide more information.

- Be on the lookout for common signs of stress such as trouble sleeping, emotional mood changes, loss of appetite, skin ailments, and stomach upsets.

- Be patient, controlled and calm in the run-up to exams. Anxiety is catching.

- Adopt a realistic attitude towards your children's abilities. Don't expect too much, but be positive and emphasise academic success rather than failures.

- Avoid comparisons with successful friends or relatives. Praise commitment as well as success and try to put the exams in perspective: they are not the be-all and end-all. Show interest in their achievements outside school work.

- Make sure there is a place available at home where the student can work alone (see pages 27–29).

- In extreme cases of stress seek professional help (see pages 164–165).

- Avoid offering rewards such as money, clothes or cars. Young people may feel they are being manipulated, and it might stop them developing an interest in the subject for its own sake.

- Above all, make it clear that your son or daughter is valued for reasons entirely unconnected with academic progress.

- Read **Saying helpful and unhelpful things** (pages 167–168) and spot your most helpful sayings.

TALKING ABOUT YOUR PROBLEM

Ask your helper to be an attentive listener for you. Negotiate the kind of help you would like. Here are two suggestions for you to consider.

Listening without speaking
Ask your partner to say nothing, simply give you their undivided attention. Ask them to encourage you to talk by non-verbal signals, e.g. smiles, nods, eye contact, touch, and to allow you to display any emotion you feel.

Talk for as little or as long as you like about any aspect of the problem that is uppermost in your mind. You could use parts of the book to give a focus to what you say, if you prefer. The exercise will give you an opportunity to listen to yourself. At the end, you could summarise the main concerns you have expressed.

Listening and summarising
Use the above negotiated approach, asking your helper to be equally attentive and encouraging to you. This time, leave pauses in what you say and express, for your helper to summarise both the fact and the feeling in what you have said. If the helper doesn't summarise the essential meaning of what you have said, help by repeating what you

expressed and giving your helper another chance to summarise it, in turn. Continue, using this approach, until you have been able to express all of the problem.

Tackling the problem

Use your helper to work through the four stages of the **Tackling the problem** exercise (pages 127–128) by using either of the approaches from these two **Listening** exercises (above). The helper works with you, one stage at a time, to enable you to clarify what you can do about it and how you are going to do so. You could use the same approach to talk through the **hierarchy of anxiety** (pages 128–129).

Using revision cards with a partner

Draw a diagram, make up a spider or patterned note card(s) or construct some linear key word notes.

Revise the card(s) for 15 or 20 minutes (at most). Re-check that you understand and can recall all of the card(s) contents.

Teach your partner about the topic, allowing – and encouraging – questions about the topic. When a point is unclear, stop and explain it. Work through the topic until you have both completed it to your satisfaction *or* have agreed to meet again to continue.

Sharing topics with a partner

Example

Cathy used one other friend on the course to revise with, by dividing up topics, revising them individually, and then meeting to discuss them. What happened in the discussion was that fresh questions and issues arose which led to both further revision and further enquiry. It worked for both of them.

Using your partner to fire questions

Work for a set period in your work room, e.g. half to one hour. Then ask your co-operative partner to fire questions at you about the topic. It will obviously help if the partner had some knowledge about the topic or a clear indication of what to ask. However, what you are seeking from this exercise is to keep flexible and be alert to surprise questions. Fresh angles are a bonus from this method.

Using someone to test you

An additional option for **Using a basic revision method** (pages 63–64) is to explain what you have been reading and learning to your partner. Alternatively, pass your partner your notes and ask to be tested on your understanding. 'Test me' is one of the commonest forms of using others as helpers and is as useful as it ever was.

USING MORE THAN ONE HELPER FOR REVISION

Conducting a seminar

One person in a group of 3, 4, 5 or 6 explains a topic to others. They can then ask questions, debate your points, give their own ideas, etc.

This technique has been very successful for a number of students I know and is highly recommended by them.

You can use this idea of marking and commenting on each other's work in a number of ways:

- On presentations to a seminar.

- On introductions or conclusions to a topic, written or spoken.

- On the clarity and evidence of revision notes, particularly **Key word revision cards** (pages 64–68). (NB most cards are prepared for yourself. They may need amendment for presentation to others.)

- On short or outline answers to questions. A photocopy of each, marked silently, marks announced and then discussed, is particularly effective. (Examiners use the same techniques when they meet at standardisation meetings to ensure they are marking in the same way, to the same standard and have grasped all the points for which marks may be awarded.)

Using brainstorming

Choose a topic or question which has a large number of aspects to it. Questions involving solutions, consequences, results or which ask you to offer explanations are particularly appropriate.

In your group, negotiate for one person to record information for the group. This may be on a tape recorder, a linear note form or patterned notes on a large sheet of paper or a piece of A4 paper. The recorder has the essential role of recording every point made by other group members.

Each member of the group, including the recorder, now has the opportunity to offer their solutions, explanations, etc. The ideas should come as quickly as possible. All of them must be recorded no matter how absurd or funny another group member may find them. No member of the group is allowed to criticise another member's ideas. The recorder should intervene if this happens and stop the rule breaker. Once all the ideas are recorded (the recorder can give interim summaries of what has been written down if this method is being used) the whole list can be opened up for debate and criticism and evaluation. In this way, all the ideas have been heard before any evaluation occurs and a wider perspective has been thrown on the question.

You can brainstorm by yourself too. A tape recorder or blank sheet of paper is all you need to note down all you know or want to know of a topic.

Giving a five-minute lecture

Prepare your topic by listing the major points you would wish to make in answer to a question. Talk about them, briefly, without elaboration, detail, detour or examples for exactly five minutes.

Invite your group to ask questions. Each member may ask only one question at a time, in turn. You should make your answers brief – one word, one phrase, one sentence answers. The object is to maximise participation and to generate a large number of questions and thus stimulate every member's thinking about the topic.

Forming your own revision group

One mature student, Tilly, was a member of a seminar group on the second year of her degree course. They were extremely helpful to each other, forming a revision group and tackling topics together in the period before the exam.

A prize-winning student in Trinidad worked as part of a group of eight students throughout the revision session and attributed part of her success to the group.

Both groups used the approaches mentioned both in this chapter and in chapters 3 and 4.

Pooling your questions

When you meet as a group, one idea is to agree that you will say what individual questions you are concerned to tackle. As it is important to frame your concerns as questions, not just as 'worries', everybody may need to say what their worry-of-the-moment is and then be asked to frame it as a question.

As each question is asked in turn, others give you their ideas, suggestions or answers to the question. You can make the best use of the time if everybody listens to the answers to someone else's question (which may be equally relevant to their own). Make sure everybody has the chance to have their questions heard, even if they do not immediately get fully answered. You and they can always have another go next time you meet.

Glossary

Assessor. A qualified person responsible for carrying out assessments. Widely used as a term in relation to the person responsible for assessing NVQs.

Assignment. Any task given to you to complete as part of a course. It will usually be marked and the outcome count in some way towards your final assessment for the year.

Awarding body. Any body which operates the assessment of a programme of study and/or awards the qualification. Examples are City and Guilds, GCSEs, Royal Society of Arts and specific universities, who award 'their own qualifications'.

Brainstorming. A way of tackling a problem either in a group or individually, which encourages the widest range of ideas to hammer out, without criticism. The process of evaluating their usefulness comes later.

Continuous assessment. The process of gaining marks from a course other than by examination. Assessment can both give you a guide to your progress and count towards your final year result. Can be tests, essays, reports, projects. Can also be combined with exams.

Coursework. Any assignments or tasks you set yourself to do either in college, school or at home. In school it is often referred to as 'homework' when it is not completed in class time.

Deadline. A date or time of day by which a piece of coursework, project or assignment is required to be submitted.

Dissertation. A major written assignment often completed in later, particularly final, years of undergraduate courses of study. Usually a substantial piece of work involving some information-gathering or survey. Can also be undertaken in postgraduate study.

GCSE. General Certificate of Secondary Education.

Kinaesthetic. The sense of touch, feel and movement.

Neuro-linguistic programming (NLP). A method and process for discovering the patterns, skills and techniques used by outstanding individuals in any field to achieve outstanding results.

Open University (OU). The world's leading distance learning university offering a wide range of study programmes including degrees and postgraduate studies, with high quality materials to accompany them.

Portfolio. A collection of evidence to prove competence against standards and/or to illustrate the wide range of work you have accomplished.

Professional courses. Specialist training courses at various levels, including postgraduate level, designed to produce greater levels of vocational competence as well as to update skills and know-how.

Programme of study. A term used to cover any course or unit of study at any level of education or training.

Project. Any usually larger assignment which involves some investigation, information-gathering or creative design on your part.

RSA. Royal Society of Arts, a long-established body involved in the development of a wide range of skills in learning and in competence.

Scottish National Vocational Qualification (S/NVQ). Qualifications designed by industry lead bodies to develop vocational qualifications at five levels for everyone in the industry – from new staff to senior personnel.

Semester. A period of study used in universities, in preference to 'terms', to incorporate a programme of study. Examinations are frequently incorporated within the semester. There are likely to be two or three semesters in an academic year.

Seminar. Traditionally an opportunity for a small group to discuss issues raised by one member of the group, in the form of a 'paper' on a topic or a presentation. A tutor is present who may choose to take a large or small part each week. The 'small' group may consist of over 25 people on some courses, but hopefully it would be between ten and 15 at most.

Synthesis. A fusing together of different senses, ideas or skills into a whole.

TEC. Training and Enterprise Councils are responsible on a regional basis for effective training in the 1990s.

Undergraduate. Anyone studying for a first degree, BA, BSc, BEng, BEd and so on, as well as someone studying for a Higher Diploma (although they are also termed Diplomates).

Workshop. There tend to be two ways in which this word is used. One is to describe a place where creative design or fabrication takes place in arts and technology fields. The other is to describe a meeting in which you will be asked to participate in practical ways such as talking in pairs, writing down ideas, dramatising events or learning practical relaxation techniques.

Further Reading

BOOKS

Ansell, Gwen, *Make the Most of Your Memory*, National Extension College 1984. Looks at all aspects of memory in a clear, practical way.

Ashman, S. and George, A., *Study and Learn*, Heinemann 1982. Highly recommended.

Barnes, R., *Successful Study for Degrees*, Routledge 1992. One of a number of books recommended by students as being helpful.

Bourner, T. and Race, P., *How to Win as a Part-Time Student*, Kogan Page 1990. For those tackling study in what can be a very difficult way, a helpful book to guide you through.

Bowness, Charles, *The Practice of Meditation*, Aquarian Press 1979. A useful book with a lot of meditative techniques to help you unwind.

Buzan, Tony, *Use Your Head*, BBC Publications 1989. Very good on creative patterns and certain kinds of memorising.

Buzan, Tony, *Use Your Perfect Memory*, Plume-Penguin 1991. Useful ideas on improving your memory.

Castro, Miranda, *The Complete Homeopathy Handbook*, Macmillan. Available by post from The Homeopathic Supply Co., Fairview, 4 Nelson Road, Sheringham, Norfolk NR26 8BU.

Chapman, David, *GCSEs: surviving the course*, Dextral Books. Practical tips on tackling GCSEs.

Davies, Don, *Maximising Examination Performance: A Psychological Approach,* Kogan Page 1986. This book reports the result of a survey of stress-related problems of post-A level students, and suggests some ways to do the psychological preparation for exams.

Dunleavy, P., *Studying for a Degree – in the Humanities and Social Sciences*, Macmillan 1986. A very detailed and helpful book for some of the detailed issues of studying especially in writing critically and structuring work.

Edwards, Dorothy, *Drawing on the Right Side of the Brain*, Souvenir

Press 1981. Looks at ways of using the creative, free-flowing mental faculties and includes some very helpful ideas, together with a step-by-step course.

Fairbairn, G. and Winch, C., *Reading, Writing and Reasoning: A Guide for Students*, Open University Press 1991. Another book recommended to me by students as a help to improving the analysis of a question and the quality of argument.

Freedman, M. and Hawkes, J., *Yoga at Work*, Element Books 1996. 10-minute yoga workouts for working or studying situations such as sitting on a chair, with clear illustrations and instructions.

Freeman, R., *Mastering Study Skills*, Macmillan 1982. Includes some useful guidelines on thinking and arguing effectively.

Hennessy, B., *Writing an Essay*, How To Books 1994. A popular guide to tackling coursework essays.

Jensen, E., *Super Teachng*, Turning Point Publishing 1995. (ISBN 0-9637832-0-3.) An American book packed with practical ideas on how to incorporate the latest understandings of learning into teaching.

Lorayne, H., *Improve Exam Results in 30 days*, Thorsons 1992. Some highly specific and wide ranging memory tips on such issues as learning formulae.

Madders, J., *Stress and Relaxation: Self-Help Techniques for Everyone*, (1988 edition). Macdonald Optima.

Marshall, L. and Rowland, F., *Guide to Learning Independently*, OU Press 1993. A useful all-round study guide with useful chapters on dissertations.

Northedge, A., *Good Study Guide*, Open University Press 1990. An excellent general resource about study skills aimed primarily at adults.

O'Connor, J. and Seymour, J., *Introducing Neuro-Linguistic Programming*, Mandala 1990.

Race, P. and Bourner, T., *How to Win as a Part-Time Student: Study Skills Guide*, Kogan Page 1990. Another useful guide for the part-time student.

Rose, Colin, *Accelerated Learning*, Accelerated Learning Systems Ltd. Fifth edition 1991.

Rowntree, D., *Learn How to Study*, 1996. One of the best books published on studying tech-niques in a programmed text form. Very good guidelines on taking examinations.

Smith, A., *Accelerated Learning in the Classroom*, Network Educational Press Ltd 1996. A useful overview of some of our developing understanding of how we learn, written for teachers to apply in the classroom.

Smith, P., *Writing an Assignment*, How To Books 1997. Useful guidelines to help with coursework.

Wilson, D., *Instant Calm*, Penguin 1995. Packed with ideas for relaxing the mind and body in different situations; many ideas similar to those contained in this book.

Wilson, P., *The Little Book of Calm*, Penguin 1996. Another of Paul Wilson's best-selling handy-sized books for pocket or bag – with one calming idea a page.

AUDIO/VIDEO TAPES

Davies, Don, *How to Conquer Exam Nerves: Maximising Examination Performance*. Available by post from Performance Programmes, 16a Priory Road, Malvern, Worcester WR14 3DR. This 64-minute tape covers test anxiety; anxiety stress and performance; learning to relax; developing confidence; improving concentration and increasing efficiency.

Letts Study Guides: GCSE; A/AS level; languages – including audio cassettes. A series of commercially produced GCSE and A Level study packs which can help with individual subjects.

'Lingo'. Examines how to learn a language. BBC Publications 1991.

Longman Revise Guides, GCSE and A level. Specific subject guides.

Longman GCSE Pass Packs. Using an audio-tape plus booklet on subjects like English, Physics etc.

Wright, C., *The Exam Kit*, Letts Educational/Channel 4 1996. A very practical useful guide and video produced to accompany a Channel 4 programme for students tackling GCSE. Order from Channel 4, England (see Useful Addresses).

Useful Addresses

Accelerated Learning Systems Ltd, 60 Aylesbury Road, Aston Clinton, Aylesbury, Buckinghamshire. Produce an excellent study guide as well as packs of material to learn languages. Printed, audio and video materials of high quality.

Association of University and College Counsellors (AVCC), c/o British Association for Counselling, 1 Regent Place, Rugby, Warwickshire CV21 2PJ. Tel: (01788) 550899. For locating counselling help in college and university.

Channel Four Schools, PO Box 100, Warwick CV34 6TZ. Tel: (01926) 433333. Fax: (01926) 450178. Ordering the Exam Kit by credit card: Tel: (01926) 436444. Video £9.99, Guide £6.95.

Society of Homeopaths, 2 Artizan Road, Northampton NN1 4HU. Tel: (01604) 21400. Will provide a list of homeopaths in your area.

Index

abbreviations, 69–70
ability, 16, 17, 18, 108
achievement, 17–18
anchoring, 159–160
answers (*see* questions)
anxiety, 124–166
asking questions (*see* questions)
association (*see* memory)
audio-tape, 29, 31, 63, 68, 73, 83, 89–90, 91, 94, 172, 178

brain, right and left halves, 78–79
brain patterns, creative (*see* notes)
brainstorming, 172–173
breathing techniques (*see* relaxation)
brief tips, 21, 45, 72, 96, 125

colours, 34–35, 81, 83, 85, 92–94, 161–163
computers, 41–43, 54–55
concentration, 26–27
corpse, the, 147
'Cosmo day', 41
counselling, 23, 164
coursework, 20–43

deadlines, 20, 21, 40–41, 174
determination, 16–18
diary, 58
disability, 99–100
dissertation, 32
drinking, 18, 141, 143–144

dyslexic students, 99–100

e-mail, 43
energy, 26
equipment, 100-101
essays, 30, 42, 104, 117–119
exam 'nerves', 124, 134–136
examinations, 95–124
    oral exams, 121
    past experience of, 127

feelings, 14, 18, 127, 136–140
filing, 29–30
folders, 30
friends, 18, 33, 44, 105, 165, 167, 168–169

GANNT chart, 36
GCSE, 8, 20, 32, 95, 104–105, 108, 174, 178
Gestalt idea, 35–36

hard work, 20, 21
health, 96, 99–100
help, 43, 164–165
helpers, 164–165, 167–170
hierarchies,
    revision, 47–50
    anxiety, 128–129
hugging, 157–158

imagination, 88, 92, 160–164
interest, 12, 17, 47–50, 51
Internet, 43

journal, learning, 31–32
juggling, 144–145

key word revision cards, 64–68
key words, 64, 113–114, 114–116

lectures, 173
  five minute, 173
legibility, 122
libraries, 19
listening, 170–171
  focused, 164
  importance of, 170–171
  to music, 19
lists, 47, 52–53, 128–129

mathematics, 92–94
massage, 145
memory, 71–94
  association, 73
  better, 75
  mnemonics, 88–89
  recalling, 61, 76–77
  repeating, 73
  testing, 74
motivation, 16–18, 21, 23–24,
  25, 33–34
multiple choice (see questions)
music, 19

negative,
  attitudes, 105, 107–8, 133–134
  self-statements, 133–134
  symbols, 48, 49
neuro-linguistic programming,
  174
notebook, 58
notes,
  filing, 68
  mind-map, 56–57
  patterned, 55–56, 114
  spider, 54, 114
  use in revision, 53–56
NVQ, 32

objective tests (see questions)
Open University, 69, 76
outline answers, 15–16, 112,
  113–114

panic, 139–140, 149
parents, 105, 167, 169–170
performance, 17–18, 102–105,
  122–123
photograph album, 35
portfolios, 31, 175
positive,
  attitudes, 133–134
  symbols, 149–150
  talk, 24–25
Post-its, 34
problems,
  tackling, 127–128, 171
  talking about, 170–172
projects, 32, 33, 127–128, 164–
  165

quotes, 136
questions,
  analysing your questions, 15–
    16, 22
  around a topic, 12–13, 52–53
  importance of, asking, 12–16
  making up, 14–15, 26
  multiple choice, 119–120
  objective, 119–120
  practice answers to, 173
  spotting, 51–52
  types of, 12–16, 114–116
  underlining key words in, 15–
    16

raps, 89–90
reading,
  with questioning approach,
    12–16
  the exam paper, 110–112
recalling (see memory)
relaxation,
  breathing, 141, 149–152

emergency technique, 149
muscular, 152–159
rest and relax, 27
visualisation, 160–164
remembering (*see* memory)
Rescue Remedy, 140
retreat (*see* sanctuary)
reviewing, 44, 46, 75–76
revision, 44–70, 173
basic method, 63–64
rewards, 25, 110

sanctuary, 138–139
saunas, 149
science and technology subjects,
91–94
self statements, 130–136
seminars, 172, 175
senses, using, 79–88
simulation, 126
sleep, 27, 142–147
spelling, 122
stress, 124–140
summarising, 170–171
symbol system, 48, 49, 51

talisman, 166

teachers, 104
testing, 74, 102
television, 19, 69
time, use of, 31
in coursework, 31, 36–40
in exams, 110–113
in revision, 58–61
topics,
spotting, 50, 51
subjects and symbols, 47–51
treats (*see* rewards)
tutors, 23, 33

understanding, 44, 47–50, 63,
71–73, 92

variety, 27, 45
video, 69
visualisation, 160–163
visual recall, 79, 80, 81, 82–83,
85–88

waking, 140–141
where to study, 27–30, 136–139
work rate, 16–18
worry (*see* anxiety)